SAVING
ONE NATION
UNDER GOD

God bless America!

Tricia Raymond

SAVING ONE NATION UNDER GOD

The Role of the Pledge of Allegiance in
America's Fight Against Socialism

by

TRICIA RAYMOND

Liberty Aloud Books

www.libertyaloud.com

Published by Liberty Aloud Books, Madison, MS

Library of Congress Cataloging-in-Publication Data has been applied for.

Saving One Nation Under God, The Role of the Pledge of Allegiance in America's Fight Against Socialism may be purchased for educational, business, or sales promotional use. For information, please email libertyaloud@gmail.com

ISBN: 978-0-9798301-1-2

First Printing—November 2011

http://www.libertyaloud.com

This book is printed on acid free paper.

Cover design by Michael Merck

Front cover photograph by Hubert Worley

Interior design by Ken and Tricia Raymond

Logo design by Michael Raymond

"ONE GENERATION SHALL PRAISE THY

WORKS TO ANOTHER AND SHALL DECLARE

THY MIGHTY ACTS."

PSALM 145:4

CONTENTS

PREFACE

I would like to share with my readers my motivation for writing this book. More than any other reason, I wrote it because I love America and I care about her future. We live in a time in which Americans from all backgrounds are concerned that our children and grandchildren will not grow up in the same country we grew up in. If there is anything Americans can unite on today, it is that we are a nation divided. I think we can also agree that a "house divided will not stand."

In researching the history of the Pledge of Allegiance, I discovered that America has been down the road of divisiveness before. And although it may sound simplistic, our patriotism has always been the primary force that brought us back again to the land of unity.

Am I so naïve to think that the Pledge of Allegiance alone can unite America? Certainly not. The issues we face today are far too complex and complicated. But, equally so, have we become so sophisticated that we no longer realize the significance of our patriotic traditions in getting us through such discordant times?

It gives me hope to know that Americans have faced monstrous issues before—the Civil War and the fight for Civil Rights to name two of the most important—and come out victorious. But, it grieves me to realize that the one foundational element that cemented us together during those times is disappearing, that is, a strong belief in, respect for and acknowledgement of the Judeo Christian belief system throughout our nation's history.

Which brings me to the point of this book. Saving "one nation under God" in the Pledge of Allegiance is at the very core of saving one nation under God. President Ronald Reagan captured this thought much better than I have when he said in one of his many speeches supporting the role of religion in government, "A State is nothing more than a reflection of its citizens."

I truly believe that those who seek to remove "under God" from the Pledge of Allegiance are simply louder than the rest of us who believe it should stay. I also believe that the best way to combat their often cacophonous arguments is to live life loudly as one *individual* under God. Having said that, one of the most practical ways to put this into action is to learn the history of the Pledge of Allegiance. And then, pass it along to your children and grandchildren, nieces and nephews, co-workers and family. If we, this generation of Americans, do not successfully pass along to the next generation a love for America and an accurate record of our heritage, America will surely die.

God is and always has been at the very center of American government and culture. It is part of our heritage as a nation. Hopefully, it will remain part of our future as well.

Four score and seven years ago, our fathers brought forth
upon this continent, a new nation, conceived in liberty ...
—Abraham Lincoln, Gettysburg Address, November 19, 1863

Discourage the teaching of American history
— Communist goal #31

ONE

FOR THE LOVE OF LIBERTY

The history of the Pledge of Allegiance began in 1888, when two seemingly unrelated events entered the stage of American history and forever influenced our national culture. No historian has ever connected these two events, although many have mentioned the significance of one, the appearance of the futuristic novel, *Looking Backward, 2000-1887,* on the best-selling list for 1888. *Looking Backward* is a utopian novel with a romantic twist in which the main character, Julian West, goes to sleep May 30, 1887, and wakes up September 10, 2000, to an America that has become completely Socialist.

1

Written by a little-known journalist, Edward Bellamy, it sold more than one million copies over the next two years. Prior to Bellamy's book, Socialism, Communism, and anarchy were not topics typically chatted about around nineteenth-century water coolers. But Bellamy found a way to successfully pique the curiosity of millions of Americans by weaving a science fiction storyline in a distant time around an otherwise dry and academic subject—running a government. By doing so, he brought the topic of Socialism to the American public—and later, the world—like no other writer ever had.[1]

As a result, interest in Socialism exploded. Bellamy Clubs, also called First Nationalist Clubs, popped up around the country as small groups of idealistic Americans attempted to plan the nationalization of industry and the redistribution of wealth among the classes. Patterned after the British Fabian Socialist Society, Nationalist Clubs believed in a slow, non-revolutionary imposition of Socialism, using political action, propaganda, and when necessary, deceit, to reach their goal.[2]

Among those who helped develop the newly formed Nationalist Clubs was Edward's cousin, Francis Bellamy. Few readers will recognize the names of either Edward or Francis, but readers of this book will be interested to learn that Francis Bellamy, at that time a Baptist minister by profession, is the man credited with having written the Pledge of Allegiance.

In October of 1888, the second significant event unfolded—an advertisement in the sale section of the nation's most popular family magazine of its day, *The Youth's Companion*. By all appearances, it was nothing more than an ad to sell American flags. In reality, it was a call to action. The creator of the ad, James Upham, an editor with *The Youth's Companion*, beseeched parents, teachers, and community leaders to inspire younger Americans to love their country and to hold dear the freedoms that had been passed on to them. "Could the Stars and Stripes be hung upon the walls of every home and of every school room in the land, how grandly might patriotism and love of liberty be unceasingly taught," Upham wrote in the *Companion* ad.

The Youth's Companion, October 25, 1888

This advertisement was the genesis of a historic and long-lasting patriotic movement in America. It was out of this movement that the Pledge of Allegiance was born, creating a legacy that has lasted to this day.

The concurrence of Bellamy's book, a phenomenon that revealed America's initial curiosity about Socialism, and Upham's advertisement, an effort to inspire patriotism in young Americans, sets the stage for the telling of the history of the Pledge of Allegiance. For, although Upham's advertisement was in no way a reaction to Bellamy's book, it was, indeed, a response to growing tension throughout the nation over Bellamy's subject matter—an America that chooses Socialism over Capitalism, government control over individual freedom.

James Upham's desire to encourage patriotism in a young generation of Americans did not arise from a vacuum. Americans were concerned about the future of the nation. And for good reason. For while this period of history was one of the most exciting in terms of industrial progress and growth, it was also one of the most tumultuous in terms of national identity and security.

After the Civil War, the Industrial Revolution came crashing into the lives of Americans, bringing with it mind-boggling inventions, discoveries, and changes. Over half a million patents were issued in the latter half of the 1800s. That was more than ten times what had been granted in the previous half century.[3] Every aspect of life was affected, not the least of which was work itself.

America was becoming less and less a nation of small businessmen working as farmers, tradesmen, or craftsmen. They were now employees working for a paycheck in a factory. In the transition, the uncomplicated relationship that had long existed between a man and his work seemed to be coming to an end.

Also coming to an end was an American landscape dotted with family farms and small towns. This was the era in which cities grew at phenomenal rates—both the number of them and the number of people living in them. In the early 1800s, scarcely six percent of Americans lived in cities. By the late 1880s, that figure had grown to nearly thirty percent.[4] Chicago doubled in size between 1880 and 1890. Milwaukee grew tenfold between 1850 and 1890. By the end of the 1800s, New York, Philadelphia, and Chicago each had a population of over one million people[5], unheard of throughout most of civilization, especially for a nation as young as America. In a relatively short amount of time, America became a nation of people condensed in industrial cities, rather than dispersed throughout the countryside on small, independent farms.

Of course, the population boom in cities was helped significantly by millions of immigrants flocking to America's shores to escape war, disease, or famine in their native countries. But no longer did they come seeking land to farm. Cities were the new land-of-milk-and-honey, and along with scores of native-born Americans, immigrants flooded into them in search of work.

It was not only the explosion of city populations with their accompanying problems of overcrowding, filth, and lack of infrastructure that concerned Americans. It was also the shift of influence from close-knit farming communities to huge industrial centers that disquieted our nineteenth-century ancestors. As millions of families left farming to pursue factory jobs in cities, the center of power, activity, and ideas shifted as well.

This was no small matter because it put the issue-of-all-nineteenth-century-issues right up there front and center, the annoying problem that every nativist American has had to confront and that every academic has harped on since the turn of the eighteenth century—immigration, or more specifically, America's response to immigration.

It goes without saying that the vast majority of immigrants came to America with the intention of becoming productive American citizens, loyal to their new nation and willing to follow the laws, learn the language, and assimilate into the American culture. And few would argue that certain immigrant groups experienced undeserved discrimination and sometimes violence as they arrived in their adopted country.

But it is equally important to recognize the undeniable fact that *some* immigrants came to America openly espousing a desire to violently overthrow the American government and replace it with a form of Socialism, a concept initiated by Europeans, who, starting in the 1840s, transported the idea to America. It stands to reason that native-born Americans were uneasy about this new concept seeping into America's culture, literature, education, and politics. It wasn't *always* the immigrant that Americans were suspicious of. But it was *often* the Socialist tendencies they brought with them that caused concern. And legitimately so.

By 1888, the revolutionary ideas of Socialism, Communism, and anarchy had taken root in Europe and

Russia. Many revolutionaries who had fought to overtake their governments came to America to do the same here. When these immigrants arrived, they settled in cities, where they had access to millions of people, many of whom had just arrived themselves and did not yet know the ways of America's government.

An example of such a revolutionary was Johann Most. Born in Germany, Most is best known for "fueling the growth and militancy of the American anarchist movement."[6] After serving a stint in a German prison for his part in organizing Socialist activities, Most traveled to London to agitate there. In 1881, when he learned that the Russian czar had been assassinated, Most openly expressed his delight by exhorting his fellow anarchists to assassinate even more leaders.

That bought him another prison term, this time in London, where he was sentenced to hard labor. During this time, Most became a martyr to the cause and gained notoriety as a relentless anarchist who would stop at nothing to start a revolution. Released from prison in 1882, he immediately made his way to Chicago to get involved in the anarchist movement there. He readily volunteered his acquired skills at revolutionary tactics and violence to help build the young anarchist movement into a power worth reckoning with. "No country in the world is to-day so well prepared for anarchist agitation as America," Most wrote in an 1890 pamphlet titled *The Social Monster: A Paper on Communism and Anarchism.*[7] With very little publicity, he drew a crowd of six thousand people the first time he spoke in America.[8] "The existing system will be quickest and most radically overthrown by the annihilation of its exponents. Therefore, massacres of the enemies of the people must be set in motion,"[9] he later said.

Below is an excerpt taken from a newspaper article about Johann Most after his death.

Arrested Many Times

In New York Most served several terms in jail. Finally on April 26, 1886, he addressed a mass meeting urging workmen to arm themselves and prepare for battle. He was sentenced to a year in prison and served his term.

During his career Most visited many of the large cities of the country to make anarchist speeches and was arrested many times. His last notable arrest was in September, 1901 when he was convicted for publishing an article in his newspaper, *Die Freiheit*, declaring it no crime to kill a ruler. The article appeared the day after President McKinley was shot at Buffalo. For this article he served two months in jail.[10]

Most's story is hardly unique. Dozens of other anarchist and Socialist immigrant leaders in America at this time were equally dedicated to the utter destruction of the American system of government. George Schilling, Adolph Fischer, George Engle, Albert Spies, Samuel Fielden, Friedrich Sorge, Emma Goldman, Andrew Berkman, Paul Grottkau, and Michael Schwab are the names of some. They joined dozens of American-born Socialists and anarchists, devotees such as Albert Parsons, convicted of conspiracy and hanged for his role in the Haymarket Riot, America's first bomb attack. Each of these individuals was either directly or indirectly involved in violent strikes, assassinations, and assassination attempts, inciting riots and various other activities directed at fomenting revolution in America.

The anarchists' success stories are written in the annals of history: The Railway Strike of 1877, the Great Southwest Railroad Strike of 1886, the Riot at McCormick Reaper Works in 1886, the Haymarket Riot of 1886, the Homestead Strike of 1892, the Pullman Strike of 1893, and the Seattle General Strike of 1901. These were some of the notable strikes among the thousands—

yes, thousands—that occurred nationwide during the last three decades of the 1800s. In 1886 alone, over fifteen hundred strikes occurred in the nation, involving more than half a million workers.[11] In 1919, there were over thirty-six hundred strikes, involving over four million workers.[12]

The words "strike" and "labor unrest" hardly begin to describe the violence associated with these incidents. In reality, they turned industrial cities into isolated war zones, sometimes coming very near to all-out class warfare. Armed Americans—militias, laborers, and Pinkerton guards—maimed, wounded, and killed one another. One or more agitators, mostly Socialists or Socialist sympathizers, provoked each incident, using the anger of laborers (and there is no argument that the laborers had legitimate complaints worth fighting for) to incite revolution in the streets with the goal of overthrowing the American government.

In short, the waning decades of the nineteenth century found America to be a nation divided. Although the Civil War had ended twenty-three years earlier, its bitter wounds kept America a fractured nation—united on paper, but separated in spirit. Industrial management was pitted against laborers, while both sides figured out how to adapt to the breathtaking changes occurring all around them. Native-born Americans were anxious about the millions of immigrants pouring into the country.

But the overarching issue that most unnerved Americans during this period was the introduction of radical ideologies that attacked American principles of government and way of life. Liberty was facing an enemy it had never faced before, and Americans didn't like it. They worried that the freedom they enjoyed would be lost by the time their own children reached adulthood. In 1888, the future of America seemed to be on the minds of nearly everyone.

That is why the advertisement suggesting the American flag be flown in every home and schoolroom was the right idea at the right time. James Upham's vision to fly a flag in front of every school in America, simplistic as it was, would be a visible reminder of national unity, prompting all who passed to think about the "honor and glory of our native land."[13]

... we feel a profound respect for these United States, and for the brave men who in the days of the Revolution dared to risk their lives and fortunes that America might be a free land.
— Lesson from *A Patriotic Primer for the Little Citizen,* 1909

Discredit the American founding fathers. Present them as selfish aristocrats
— Communist goal #30

TWO

FLAGS UNFURLED, PATRIOTISM RENEWED

When the first ad to sell American flags appeared in *The Youth's Companion,* James Upham had no way of knowing if his idea would strike a chord of interest or die for lack of it. For fifteen months, *The Youth's Companion* subscribers did not see another advertisement to sell flags. But on January 9, 1890, the second ad appeared, and *Companion* readers discovered that there were thousands of like-minded Americans who supported the idea of flying a flag in front of their school. What would ultimately come to be known as the Schoolhouse Flag

Movement was officially underway.

Under the title "The Flag and the Public Schools," James Upham wrote, "*The Youth's Companion*, in one of its issues of more than a year ago, set forth the idea of the Flag and the Public Schools. The idea is becoming popular, and the American Flag can now be seen floating over many a patriotic school."[14]

THE FLAG
And the Public Schools.

Our offer of presenting a 9x15 Bunting Flag, 42 stars, to one school in each of the 42 States, has awakened great interest. (See offer in the issue of THE COM-PANION for January 9th.)

The State of Minnesota has the honor of sending in the first essay. We now extend this offer so as to include each of the Territories as well as each of the States.

PERRY MASON & COMPANY,
41 Temple Place,   **Boston, Mass.**

The Youth's Companion, February 20, 1890

In subsequent ads, Upham created the first of three promotions to keep the momentum going and to give students a way to acquire a flag at little or no cost—a contest in which students were invited to write an essay on patriotism and the flag.

In the next issue, an article titled "The School Flag" followed up on the growing trend of flying flags in front of schools. Readers were encouraged to raise money to purchase flags, priced from five to fifteen dollars, a sum that was easy to raise in almost any town of the United States. Guidelines were published to address such concerns as handling the flag. It was suggested that Flag Committees be formed, "composed of the head boy of each class in the school. This plan would give a committee of five, at the most."[15]

The article suggested patriotic holidays and occasions on which the flag should be raised, such as George Washington's birthday and the admission of a state into the Union. Particular attention was given to propriety, and students were discouraged from raising the flag "on days that have a party or sectarian character." With Civil War wounds still festering, the following suggestions were offered when raising the flag on "great days of the late war . . . The Flag Committee will naturally be careful not to wound sectional pride, nor excite unprofitable controversy. All can join in commemorating that day of days on which President Lincoln issued his proclamation of freedom to the slaves, and that other grand day when General Grant gave back to General Lee and his exhausted troops their side-arms and their horses, and told them to go in peace and raise a crop."

"Flag-raisings" were mentioned for the first time. The popularity of the flag was growing, and spontaneous exercises to raise and lower it each day were created at schools around the country, an activity *The Youth's Companion* encouraged. "The raising of the flag just before school in the morning, and the lowering of it just after school in the afternoon, will be a lesson in history to the neighborhood. We suggest also that a little, not too much, ceremony in the raising and lowering of the flag will add to the impressiveness of the occasion."[16]

Schools in New York City had already been reciting a patriotic pledge for years. Because New York had such a large number of immigrant children attending

THE FLAG AND THE SCHOOL.

In January last *The Companion* offered as a prize to be competed for by the pupils in the public schools of each State and Territory, a United States flag. The flags, measuring nine feet by fifteen, and made of the best bunting, were to be awarded to that school in each State and Territory, one of whose pupils should submit the best essay, not exceeding six hundred words in length, upon the subject of "The Patriotic Influence of the American Flag when raised over the Public Schools."

Pupils in public schools of forty-one States and six Territories responded to this offer. The essays have been examined, the prizes awarded, and the flags sent and received; and many if not all of them have been raised over the school-houses. We give below a list of the schools and the essayists to whom the flags were awarded.

The Youth's Companion, July 3, 1890

its schools, reciting a pledge was considered a necessary

part of every student's early education. Standing at attention, with the flag held in front of the classroom, the students would first touch their foreheads, then their hearts, while reciting "The American Patriotic Salute" in unison:

"We give our heads! And our hearts!

To God! And our country!"

Next, with their right arms outstretched toward the flag, they exclaimed,

"One Country! One Language! One Flag!"[17]

As more schools flew the Stars and Stripes, students and teachers nationwide began creating simple patriotic programs to accompany the raising and lowering of the flag each day.

Lessons in patriotism were also beginning to find their way into the public school curricula of the day. One of the most popular was *A Patriotic Primer for the Little Citizen,* written by Wallace Foster and dedicated to "instructing our youth in American patriotic history."

Back cover, *A Patriotic Primer for the Little Citizen*, Wallace Foster, 1909

Compiling the primer in memory of the creator of the American Patriotic Salute, Col. George T. Balch, Foster verbalized in his Introduction the conventional thinking of the day: "It needs no argument to prove that the perpetuation of our National life and institutions can be maintained only by inculcating in the minds and hearts of the rising generation the true principles enunciated in the Constitution and the Declaration of Independence. Therefore whatever we wish to see introduced into the life of a nation must first be introduced into the life of its schools." Foster made no bones about what he felt should be introduced into the life of America: "We must increase our interest for a grateful, reverent admiration for God, our Country, our Language, and our Flag."[18]

More flag advertisements appeared in 1890. There was an ad in February, another in June, and still another in July. In October, there were two ads, and another in mid-November. Then the Christmas issue came out, and the flag ad took on a new flavor. Suddenly, the focus was not solely on selling flags. This advertisement was more like an invitation, suggesting that the schools' newly placed flags be used to celebrate the upcoming anniversary of the discovery of America.

Upham had had an epiphany. In the not too distant

22

future, the nation would mark one of its most historic anniversaries—the four-hundredth anniversary of Christopher Columbus' discovery of America.[19] As the *Companion* editor, Upham had learned that plans were underway for an Exposition in Chicago, Illinois, later referred to as the Chicago World's Fair, as a way to celebrate the anniversary. Why not link the flag campaign to the Exposition, organizing patriotic celebrations in each town's public school, with special focus on the new flags? It would allow all Americans to celebrate in their hometowns, solving the inevitable problem of excluding the millions who could not travel to Chicago for the event. Just as importantly, it would focus attention on public schools and the critical role they played in imparting patriotism to students, both American and foreign born.

With the approval of Daniel Ford, owner of *The Youth's Companion*, Upham traveled to Chicago to pitch his idea to the organizing committee.[20] Charles C. Bonney, president of the World's Congress Auxiliary to the Columbian Exposition, also wanted an event with an educational component in which all Americans could participate. Bonney, whose workload would be considerably lightened with Upham's offer, accepted.[21] Upham, on the other hand, had just volunteered a very thinly staffed *Companion* to organize what would possibly become the most extraordinary event of the nineteenth century.

While Upham settled into the realization of the enormity of the job that lay ahead of him, little did he know that just blocks from his office, a young pastor would soon face a career change and that in a matter of months, their lives would be forever linked in American history. The pastor was Francis Bellamy, at that time the minister of Bethany Baptist Church, located on the edge of the affluent neighborhood in which Daniel Ford lived. Ford, a talented businessman known for his honesty, fairness, and generosity, was the church's main benefactor. He was also a mentor and friend to Francis Bellamy.

Ford and Bellamy were unlikely candidates for a friendship, given Ford's Capitalist ventures in publishing and Bellamy's Socialist tendencies. But their common desire to serve the poor and correct the many injustices suffered by the nineteenth-century working class brought them together. As devout Christians, both men felt a moral obligation to help the downtrodden.

Daniel Ford was a self-made businessman who started in the publishing business as an apprenticed printer.[22] As a young man, he worked as a bookkeeper for the *Watchman and Reflector*,[23] a Baptist journal that published a mixture of religious and non-religious news items. This was perhaps where he gained the knowledge he would later need to run his own profitable publication.

In 1857, Ford and a business partner purchased *The Youth's Companion* from Nathaniel Willis, who had started the magazine thirty years earlier.[24] Willis was the namesake of a Boston Tea Party member who was the editor of the *Independent Chronicle*, a widely circulated newspaper that had supported American independence in 1776.[25]

At the time of Ford's purchase, the publication had barely five thousand subscribers and was basically a Sunday School paper for youngsters. Intent on maintaining its Christian character, Ford added miscellaneous content, such as short stories, biographies, and puzzles, in order to make the magazine more appealing to a wider audience. The new content, combined with Ford's keen business sense and cutting-edge promotion department, caused the paper to grow steadily.[26]

At the time of his death in 1899, the magazine had acquired over a half million subscribers, making Ford a wealthy man. Despite his wealth, he had always lived simply, and remembering how hard he had worked to reach success, he donated generously to charitable causes. Several years before he died, he paid off the church's eight-thousand-dollar mortgage.[27] At his death, more than half his fortune of two million dollars was bequeathed to the various charities supported by the Baptist Church in New England.[28]

While Ford sought to help his fellowman through voluntary private charitable giving, Francis Bellamy sought the same effect through spreading a Christian Socialist message from the pulpit. True to the Socialist creed, Bellamy wanted to do more than feed the poor; he wanted to redistribute wealth to them.

From the start of his years as a minister, Bellamy was attracted to the idea of Socialism. As early as 1876, when he gave the commencement address upon graduating from college, Bellamy promoted Socialism. In his speech titled "The Poetry of Human Brotherhood," Bellamy embraced the French Revolution as the catalyst that awakened men to the "idea of Human Brotherhood." He further stated, "From the dignity of the individual to the Brotherhood of the race was only a step . . . ."[29] The concept of Brotherhood was a recurring theme in Bellamy's later writings, where he put forth the notion that nations are not made up of "independent individuals," but of "related individuals," tied so closely "that they make together an indivisible organism" that is imbued with a "self consciousness and moral personality." He went on to state that "as the nation becomes more self-conscious, it perceives more clearly its own responsibility for the development of each individual." It was this perception that gave Bellamy the bravado to declare that, unlike Capitalists, Socialists believed in a "fearless extension of government."[30]

Ironically, the great-grandfather of cousins Edward

and Francis Bellamy was Joseph Bellamy,[31] a student and friend of Jonathan Edwards, whose preaching brought about the Great Awakening, a spiritual revival that permanently impacted colonial America and helped usher in the American Revolution. Jonathan Edwards preached sermons that focused on individual responsibility for one's decisions and actions, clearly antithetical to the idea of a nation shouldering the responsibility for the development of individuals. The concept of individual responsibility was embraced by America's Founding Fathers and became foundational to the pursuit of independence from the Crown. The equality of all men before God and the inalienable right to religious freedom were also cutting-edge concepts taught by Edwards.[32] These principles found their way into America's founding documents and are diametrically opposed to Socialist thinking.

Joseph Bellamy was an influential preacher in his own right, who also helped shape the culture of New England and early America with the message that salvation was equally available to everyone. His greatest impact, however, came from the vast number of clergy he trained and taught over the course of his lifetime, leaving an imprint for generations after his death.

In 1889, one year after his cousin's blockbuster novel hit the shelves, Francis Bellamy became a charter member of the Society of Christian Socialists, an offshoot of the Nationalist Clubs, and very soon after that, the founder and associate editor of its monthly publication, *The Dawn*. In the May, 1890, issue of *The Dawn*, readers were told that "Jesus laid down two socialistic principles as fundamentals: (1) Scrupulous care for the little ones that believe in me—the weak, who are likeliest to go under in the struggle for existence, and (2) The proportioning of burdens to ability—he that is greatest shall be the servant of all."

Bellamy was listed in *The Dawn* as a lecturer on the topic of Christian Socialism and served as the head of its Education Committee. In that role he unabashedly urged other ministers to promote the "social gospel," distribute *The Dawn*, engage with the newspapers, and begin discussion groups in their churches on Christian Socialist topics.[33] Bellamy also believed that Socialism would first be implemented in cities and then extend to the nation. He disavowed violent revolution, preferring to do battle in the arena of ideas, by means of a lecture circuit that targeted academic and religious audiences. He was willing to be patient, stating, "The intellectual leaders of Socialism are in no hurry. They have all the time there is."[34] Throughout his early writings, Bellamy always described Capitalism in a negative light, using such terms as the "law of selfishness," "abhorrent," or a "selfish system."[35]

In short, Bellamy idealistically believed that Christian Socialism would end the violent disagreements happening at that time between working people and factory owners. His sold-out enthusiasm for Socialism inevitably spilled over into his sermons. But his admonishments fell on deaf ears. The Bethany Baptist Church congregation rejected his increasingly political sermons and in April of 1891, decided not to renew the church's budget. This decision essentially forced Bellamy out of the pulpit. It was at that time and for that reason that he accepted his mentor's offer to work for *The Youth's Companion*.

Later in life, Bellamy turned dramatically from his

Socialist beliefs. In a paper that was never published, an older Bellamy set out a promotional plan for the Pledge of Allegiance to combat the "academic radicals," "revolutionary socialists," "radical newspapers," "pacifists," and others that he considered enemies of American freedom.[36] But during his youth and young-adult years, Francis Bellamy was among those who ushered Socialism into America.

Despite his political leanings, Daniel Ford recognized in Francis Bellamy the leadership skills necessary to make the public school anniversary celebration a success. He thought Bellamy was a good writer and an even better speaker. With Upham now in need of assistance to carry out the growing responsibilities associated with the anniversary, Ford hired Bellamy and placed him in Upham's promotion department.[37]

We will never know if Daniel Ford put an end to Bellamy's proselytizing or if it was simply the burden of responsibilities in his new position that kept Bellamy occupied. But after going to work for *The Youth's Companion*, Bellamy only occasionally lectured for the Society of Christian Socialists. In July, 1891, one of his last defenses of Socialism was published. "The Tyranny of All the People" was a response to an article that voiced the question burning in the minds of millions of Americans at that time: Is Socialism Desirable?

The philosophy of the school room in one generation is the philosophy of government in the next.

—Abraham Lincoln

Get control of the schools

— Communist goal #17

THREE

THE PLEDGE MAKES ITS DEBUT

In January, 1892, it was announced that *The Youth's Companion* would be the official manager of the public schools' part of the upcoming anniversary celebration. Daniel Ford assigned the responsibility of overseeing this project to Francis Bellamy. What had begun as an idea to place a flag in front of every school in America was now a nationwide event that required the coordination of every school in the country and needed support and cooperation of public officials at every level of government. The Dedication Day exercises of the World's Columbian Exposition had to be organized in nine months by an employee who had only worked at his new job for only ten months—all without the benefit of cell phones, fax machines, laptops, or GoToMeeting.com. Needless to say, Francis Bellamy had his work cut out for him.

His first task was to gain the support of the Superintendents of Education, which would give him access to each state's educational system. Since the public schools would play a prominent part of the celebration, this was easily accomplished. The next task, however, would prove more difficult. To sustain interest over the next several months, Bellamy planned what today's marketing professionals would call "earned media." He would travel to Washington, D.C., and interview members of Congress and even the President of the United States. Then throughout the following months, he would issue press releases to bring attention to the event whenever national interest lagged.

In a six-page, typewritten memo, Bellamy justified the trip to Ford: "The Dailies will publish, and comment on, what leading statesmen say. What Mr. Blaine, Mr. Cleveland, Mr. Reed, Mr. McKinley etc. think about this plan would be telegraphed everywhere, printed and commented on editorially."[38] Furthermore, this was an election year, and Bellamy wanted to capitalize on what promised to be aggressive campaign coverage between former President Grover Cleveland and the then current President Benjamin Harrison. Bellamy wanted to interview both men, enabling him to get even more mileage out of his forward-thinking publicity campaign.

And so, Bellamy traveled to Washington, D.C., stopping first in New York to secure the support of former President Grover Cleveland. Next on his schedule was a meeting with President Harrison, who had been discreetly informed of Cleveland's support. Bellamy, acting as both lobbyist and journalist, meticulously recorded President Harrison's comments, which centered on his unfailing support for public schools and patriotic lessons in classrooms. President Harrison then went on to declare, "The school is the place for education in intelligent patriotism and citizenship," giving a nod to patriotic lessons in the classroom.[39]

Eager to move on to his next presidential duty, Harrison began to close the meeting. But Bellamy had one more request—would the President issue a proclamation making the day a national holiday, and would he recommend that American citizens observe it at their local schools? Such an action required a Congressional Resolution, but Bellamy did not know that at the time. There was something else Bellamy did not know. He had ruffled Harrison's feathers with his request. The President would now be in an untenable political position by asking a Democratically controlled House to vote on a measure that would enable a Republican president to build good will with voters by giving them a day off from work, a rare occurrence in those days. Such an action any time during a president's administration was risky, but taking this action during an election year was especially so.

Bellamy instinctively knew what President Harrison did not—it would be political suicide to oppose the *Companion*'s plan. Bellamy's gut instinct ultimately paid off, but not without a great deal of anxiety in the interim.

It would take another two months before the actual Resolution was in Bellamy's hands. Amazingly, Congress had become caught up in an argument over what the actual date of Columbus' landing was—October 12 or

October 21. Die-hard legalists referenced a change from the Julian calendar to the Gregorian calendar in 1582 that readjusted the actual date to be October 21. Columbus, however, had discovered America before the Gregorian calendar existed and recorded in his journal October 12 as the actual date of landing. When the decision was made to transition to the Gregorian calendar, one day was eliminated for each of the nine decades since Columbus' discovery, thus correcting the date of America's discovery to be October 21. The arguments went back and forth, with the October 21 faction insisting that the anniversary to celebrate the discovery of America simply had to take place on the adjusted date and that no other date would satisfy them.[40]

This put *The Youth's Companion* in an embarrassing light because they had advertised the October 12 date for more than a year at this point. But to keep his plans moving forward, and because he really had no other choice, in July, 1892—just four months before the celebration was to take place—Bellamy changed the date on all promotional material to the new date, October 21.

But that was not the only problem Bellamy faced in getting the critically necessary Resolution in his hands. President Harrison, famous for being a procrastinator, held off writing it until the last possible moment. Bellamy was so concerned it would never materialize, he traveled to D.C. a second time and headed straight to the White House to move things along. As luck would have it, President Harrison had just ordered it to be drafted by the State Department. Bellamy again seized the moment and offered suggestions as to its wording. Instead of being asked to write down his suggestions, he was asked by the Third Assistant Secretary to write the entire Resolution. It was sent to the White House, signed by the President, and returned to the State Department by five o'clock the same day—just in time for Bellamy to give it to the Associated Press.[41]

Now, therefore, I, Benjamin Harrison, President of the United States of America . . . do hereby appoint Friday, October 21, 1892, the four hundredth anniversary of the Discovery of

America by Columbus, as a general holiday for the people of the United States. On that day let the people, so far as possible, cease from toil and devote themselves to such exercises as may best express honor to the Discoverer and their appreciation of the great achievements of the four completed centuries of American life.

Columbus stood in his age as the pioneer of progress and enlightenment. The system of universal education is in our age the most prominent and salutary feature of the spirit of enlightenment, and it is peculiarly appropriate that the schools be made by the people the center of the day's demonstration. Let the National Flag float over every school house in the country, and the exercises be such as shall impress upon our youth the patriotic duties of American citizenship.

In the churches and in the other places of assembly of the people, let there be expressions of gratitude to Divine Providence for the devout faith of the Discoverer, and for the Divine care and guidance which has directed our history and so abundantly blessed our people.[42]

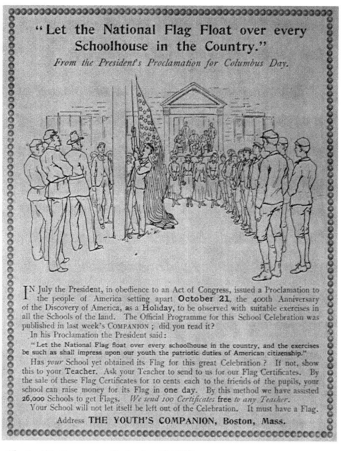

The Youth's Companion, September 15, 1892

As soon as Bellamy handed a copy of the Proclamation to the Associated Press, excitement exploded around the country. Newspapers that had previously ignored Bellamy's press releases put this one on the front page. Thirty-five of the forty-four governors issued their own proclamations. Flags were suddenly the hottest item around, and manufacturers ramped up production to keep up with demand.

But everything in the nation was not so rosy. As 1892 wore on, Americans turned their attention once again to violent strikes and another concerted push toward Socialism.

As a matter of fact, five strikes that year held the attention of the nation. During the summer months, the Coal Creek War heated up, as coal miners continued their longstanding strike against Tennessee's practice of using convict labor. After a year of fighting, dozens of men had been killed or wounded. Public sentiment swayed back and forth like the pendulum on a clock, depending on whether the militia had killed miners or *vice versa*.[43] In August, Buffalo, New York, was the site of a strike over management's refusal to follow a new state law that limited work days to ten hours. Railroad tracks were booby-trapped, and one unmanned railroad car loaded with explosives was sent roaring down the tracks to be detonated inside a train station where soldiers were disembarking.[44] No one was killed, but three of the volunteer soldiers who had been called out to bring order to the city were injured. A month earlier, violence had broken out in Idaho, when union copper miners were told that their work day would increase from nine to ten hours with no corresponding pay. Ultimately, three union miners, two company men, and one bystander were killed in the melee that followed.[45]

On November 8, the same day Grover Cleveland was re-elected President, over half the workforce in New Orleans struck, demanding increased wages, a ten-hour work day, and recognition of unions.[46] Martial law was declared, the city's electrical grid was shut off, and business came to a grinding halt. There was no violence in what came to be called the New Orleans General Strike. Ultimately, the workers' demands for a ten-hour day with increased wages were met. Their demand for union recognition, however, was left on the table.

The strike in Homestead, Pennsylvania, was pivotal. When steel workers at Andrew Carnegie's mill squared off against Pinkerton guards hired by company management, it was about more than wages, hours in a work day, and unionization. Whether through design or by accident, this strike would bring the question that both Capitalists and Socialists in America wanted brought to the forefront: Who owns property?

In 1892 the price of steel tumbled, and the predictable domino effect began anew. Management reacted by slashing wages. Labor reacted to management's reaction by striking. There was a standoff between the two sides. As was typical in these situations, there was violence. Several people were killed and injured.

But here is where the Homestead Strike was different: The workers took possession of the factory during the strike. They seemed to think they had partial ownership of it because their labor counted toward its value. In *The American Experience*, a documentary produced by Public Broadcasting, historian Paul Krause explains it this way: "Workers believed because they had worked in the mill, they had mixed their labor with the property in the mill. They believed that in some way the property had become theirs. Not that it wasn't Andrew Carnegie's, not that they were the sole proprietors of the mill, but that they had an entitlement in the mill. And I think in a fundamental way the conflict at Homestead in 1892 was about these two conflicting views of property."[47]

The two conflicting views of property were, indeed, the very crux of the matter, for it was here that Socialism and Capitalism were at war with one another. Underneath the layers of all the other conflicts this particular strike represented—the duplicity of Andrew Carnegie's public support of unions and private instructions to crush them, Henry Clay Frick's brutal and opportunistic strategy to use this strike to annihilate the union, the drama of the strongest union in the country taking on the Steel King, the assassination attempt on Frick's life by an anarchist, and the subsequent terror it caused—was found the nugget from which all strikes generate. And in America, where, for the first time in the history of civilization, everyday ordinary individuals had the opportunity to own private property, this battle was especially critical. For more than one hundred days, Americans battled Americans over these two conflicting views on a small piece of land in Pennsylvania.[48] At the end of the day, Capitalism won the Homestead battle. But the war continued to rage.

Meanwhile, Francis Bellamy's world was focused on nothing but the success of the Grand Columbus National Public School Celebration. Now that the celebration was declared an official nationwide holiday, he had to craft the actual program. Plans were to insert an Official Program in every September issue of *The Youth's Companion*, giving cities, towns, and villages across the country a guideline for their individual celebrations. Parades, color guards, speeches by local dignitaries—all of these activities could be organized according to each town's resources and level of enthusiasm. But one element was a must for everyone—a pledge around the new American flags in front of public schools. And for that to happen, a pledge had to be written.

The task fell to the two organizers, James Upham and Francis Bellamy. Both men knew the new flags had to be at center stage of the event. According to Margarette Miller, the first author to document a complete history of the Pledge of Allegiance in her book, *I Pledge Allegiance*, the men discussed their ideas over and over. But struggle as they might, neither could pen the words that appropriately expressed the meaning of the moment.

By late August, with the Public School Celebration a little over a month away, the final touches were added to the Official Program. Odes, anthems, poems, and proclamations had been written by some of the best ode, anthem, poem and proclamation writers of the day. But the task of writing a salute for the flag still remained. As a matter of fact, the first word had not yet been penned. Just two weeks remained to meet the deadline to publish the school program in *The Youth's Companion* in time for schools to begin rehearsing.

Over and over, the fatigued editors had discussed writing a salute, a vow, or a promise. The significance of the moment was as clear to them as the deadline they faced. They tossed around one idea after another, but nothing seemed to work. They discussed using one of the many different existing salutes, but they both agreed that none seemed to embody the sense of history required for so great an occasion.

As the story goes, Upham finally urged Bellamy to lock himself in his office and at the very least, draft an outline. The story continues that several hours later, Bellamy emerged with the Pledge of Allegiance scribbled on a scrap of paper.

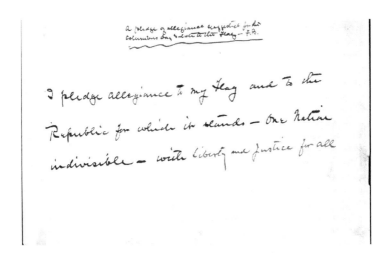

At last, the long awaited Official Program could be mailed to *The Youth's Companion*'s half-million subscribers. Tucked inside the two-page spread of flowery verbiage and high falootin' proclamations was the simply worded Pledge of Allegiance. This was its public debut—

in writing, at least. The real show stopper would be its recitation across the country in just a few weeks.

"… this is a religious people. This is historically true. From the discovery of this continent to this present hour, there is a single voice making this affirmation."
—U. S. Supreme Court,
Church of the Holy Trinity v. United States, 1892

"Eliminate prayer or any phase of religious expression in the schools on the ground that it violates the 'principle of church and state.' "
—Communist goal #28

FOUR

AMERICA UNITES AROUND THE PLEDGE

It is hard for people today to imagine the enormity of the 1892 holiday, especially one that was so completely dedicated to unabashed patriotism. The closest comparable current event is the Super Bowl. But this Columbus Day public school celebration was not about a football game. It was about America, love of country, and gratitude for liberty.

Every town, village, and city in America came out to celebrate. Many locations celebrated for the better part of a week. Droves of people attended parades, no doubt

49

eager to forget about the nation's problems and focus instead on patriotism and unity. Christopher Columbus was celebrated like a rock star. Flags flew everywhere. Bands played, and fireworks exploded. From the tiniest

These ribbons were worn by the guests of honor on October 21, 1892.

hamlets to the largest cities, Americans proudly celebrated their way of life, their heritage, and their country.

In Brooklyn, New York, half a million people gathered to watch a spectacular parade that lasted four hours and included twenty-five thousand marchers, according to the *New York Times*, October 22, 1892. In Newark, New Jersey, five thousand school children waved flags as they paraded. In San Francisco, citizens gathered at the schools to watch the presentation of the flag. Trenton, New Jersey, had the largest parade in its history, when "the Hungarian, Irish, Spanish, and French societies, along with the Grand Army of the Republic and Sons of Veterans" marched together in the celebration, as noted in the *New York Times* article. The parades surpassed all expectations in nearly every city. In Cincinnati, Ohio, the celebration parade lasted one hour and twenty minutes and a parade the day before took forty minutes to pass. Attendance at both was estimated at twenty thousand, as noted in the *St. Paul Daily Globe*, October 21, 1892. In St. Paul, Minnesota, all the schools participated, and Union veterans of the Civil War were assigned to address the students, the *Globe* stated. Even tiny Natchez, Mississippi held a "brilliant demonstration".

Chicago chose to celebrate the anniversary by dedicating the Chicago World Exposition. The much anticipated Exposition had originally been scheduled to open in 1892, but the organizers had realized early on that the 1892 deadline was too optimistic. It was decided to celebrate the anniversary by dedicating the Fair buildings instead and wait to officially open the Fair the following year. On October 20, a reported one million people crowded the streets of Chicago to watch the kick-off parade for the dedication ceremony, which was held the next day. Official counts vary, but a crowd of between 100,000 and 500,000 attended the official dedication.[49]

These were also the final days of the presidential campaign. Naturally, former President Cleveland, a current candidate, wanted a front-row seat at the parade in Chicago, where visibility in front of thousands of voters was a campaigner's dream-come-true. The President regularly rented a suite of apartments at the Hotel Victoria, which was situated along the parade route. It would have been the perfect place for campaigning and viewing, but for the unfortunate fact that the apartment was on the opposite side of the building from where the parade would pass. On October 10, the *Chicago Daily Tribune* ran an article about the President's dilemma and lamented, "At a late hour tonight the hotel people were still looking for someone who would give up his room for Mr. Cleveland's benefit, but without success."

Meanwhile, in Washington, D.C., where one would expect the most lavish celebrations to be held, the mood was anything but festive. There were, indeed, programs in the churches and schools, but the mood was somber. President Benjamin Harrison's wife, Carolyn, lay dying in the White House. Newspaper coverage of the celebrations were interspersed with daily accounts of the First Lady's condition, most of them sounding hopeless. With the President at her side, her death came four days after the anniversary.

There were celebrations in European cities, as well. *The New York Times* reported: "THE OLD WORLD'S FESTIVAL: Spain's Celebration of the Great Discovery—A Big Medieval Parade in Madrid . . . Monument unveiled at Huelva . . . Gala Performance in Berlin."[50]

In Huelva, Spain, the coastal city where Columbus sought the aid of Franciscan brothers to connect him to financiers for his voyage, the Queen Regent and her royal party attended religious services and held a reception for dignitaries. Seventeen military and other bands paraded through the streets of Madrid.[51]

In New York City, the celebration lasted an entire week. Because city officials had set the date months in advance, they celebrated on the actual day of discovery, October 12.

From *The New York Times*: "YOUNG AMERICA LEADS OFF . . . FIRST OF THE GREAT PARADES OF COLUMBUS WEEK . . . Almost 25,000 School Children and College Boys March Before Hundreds of Thousands . . . It is quite safe to say that, as a mere matter of numbers, the assemblage exceeded anything not only that has ever occurred, but that has ever been deemed possible in any American city . . . By actual count the total number of persona in the parade, including the mounted police who rode at the head of the column, the marshals, aides, musicians and members of drum corps, was 26,620. The time required for the paraders to pass a given point was two hours and fifteen minutes."[52]

It is estimated that twelve million school children recited the Pledge of Allegiance on that autumn day in October, 1892. Here is what they recited:

I pledge allegiance to my Flag,

and to the Republic for which it stands:

one Nation indivisible,

with Liberty and Justice for all.

Some people today are quick to point out that the original Pledge of Allegiance did not contain the phrase "under God." But they seldom point out that the original program instructed all public schools to acknowledge God by either a prayer or a Scripture reading immediately after reciting the Pledge.

Boston schools chose to read Psalm 145 aloud in every classroom.[53] In Salem, Massachusetts, every school in the city read from one of eight Bible verses.[54] At Lehigh University in Bethlehem, Pennsylvania, students sang, "God Bless Our Native Land."[55] The *St. Paul Daily*

Globe headlined "Religious Services and a Public Procession Important Features." Across the country in San Francisco, churches were well attended. In *The New York Times*, one journalist wrote, "It is apparent from telegraphic dispatches that Columbus Day was observed in cities, towns and villages throughout the whole country with the greatest enthusiasm. School children paraded everywhere and religious services were well attended."[56] In another *New York Times* article, it was reported that historic Trinity Episcopal Church was the site of a huge religious service. "Thousands of persons took part in the special Columbus services in Trinity Church yesterday, the throng in the afternoon especially being uncommonly large. From the magnificent candelabra flanking the chancel of the church on either hand the national colors were displayed in artistic drapings, and the American flag was festooned over each of the entrances to the building."[57]

The National Public School Celebration turned out to be one of the biggest, if not the biggest, national celebrations ever held in the history of America. Beyond all the festivities and the pageantry, Americans came

Public school in California celebrating with their new flag. October 12, 1892

together under the banner of freedom that day, as they celebrated God and country and recited for the first time a pledge designed to unite and inspire. James Upham had, indeed, united the nation around the Schoolhouse Flag.

*If destruction be our lot, we must ourselves
be its author and finisher.*

—Abraham Lincoln,
Address before the Young Men's Lyceum of
Springfield, IL, January 27, 1838

Infiltrate and gain control of more unions.

—Communist goal #36

FIVE

SOCIALISM—IN OUR OWN BACKYARD

With a renewed sense of unity, America left the 1800s behind and stepped into a promising new century. In the twelve years since the start of the Schoolhouse Flag Movement, remarkable changes had taken place. American inventors had captured the sound of voice on the telephone, motion on a movie screen, and music on a phonograph. Electricity lit up the night and powered magical machines. People could travel farther faster than at any other time in civilization. Every invention, device, mechanism, and gizmo we enjoy today—from computer screens to cell phones—went from concept to reality during this remarkable time in history.

Today, we hardly blink an eye when we talk about the Industrial Revolution. But to Americans who actually lived during this era the changes were nothing short of awe-inspiring. Equally so was the fact that these miraculous products were ever so slowly being purchased by ordinary Americans, not just the rich or the privileged. Mail order catalogs with page after enticing page of shirt collars, lampshades, and wood stoves were testament to a growing middle class. And if you had the talent or tenacity to invent, build, or innovate, America's free enterprise system allowed you to do it.

Granted, America did not yet afford everyone an equal opportunity. And many of the men who had built enormous industrial complexes had very little in the way of integrity and character. Well-documented incidents of abuse, greed, and oppression mark this period and will forever be a blot on America's history. But it should also be noted that for the first time since the Civil War, our nation again began dealing in practical terms with the idea embodied in the word "all," found in both the Declaration of Independence—"*all* men are created equal" and the Pledge of Allegiance—"with liberty and justice for *all.*" The struggle was how to continue to break down the walls so that *all* individuals could have the opportunity to pursue their God-given talents and reap the rewards for themselves, rather than for a king or a captor. It would be quite a mountain to climb. The flags and the Pledge of Allegiance had played a critical role in strengthening patriotism after two decades of malaise and divisiveness, which, in turn, allowed America to continue to refine and clarify its quest for "liberty and justice for all."

The extravagant speeches and elaborate poems that had been recited that October day in 1892 had been long forgotten. But the simple twenty-two word pledge recited around the American flag had accomplished what Upham originally hoped it would. It reinvigorated patriotism and bolstered unity. Just as importantly, it established an enduring way to pass on American values to a younger generation that would, in turn, continue to write the American story.

It was a good thing, too, because while Americans were enjoying the fruits of liberty, the menace of

Socialism had grown, both in America and abroad. Assassinations and bombings continued to shake the European continent. The Governor General of Finland was assassinated in 1904 and the King of Greece in 1913. When the Archduke of Austria was assassinated the following year, European countries were thrown into World War I, creating a turn of events that effectively led to the first Socialist victory on a national scale—the formation of Communist Russia in 1917.

Socialism in America was growing, as well. One leading Socialist recalled that prior to the publication of *Looking Backward*, the number of American Socialists could be counted on one hand.[58] But in the twelve years after the Columbus Day celebration and leading up to the turn of the century, the movement had clarified what it stood for, proselytized thousands, and purged its ranks of ne'er-do-wells. At the same time, labor conflicts continued to flare up all over the country.

The result was that a growing number of native-born Americans began leading the movement, setting a new course for successful revolution that worked "from within" to achieve its goals. This new group of Socialist pioneers was just as militant as their forbears, but focused on nonviolent strategies. Elections, union organizations, and academia were now the roads to revolutionize America. Die-hard anarchists would remain dedicated to the Marxist paradigm of class warfare. But the strategy to transform the nation would be formed by savvy Americans who understood and appreciated the power of the political system. By 1900, they began to distance themselves from violent anarchists and moved toward more benign methods of revolution.

The fact that Socialists were willing to entertain "peaceful" means of revolution did not matter a whit to the American public. In their minds, turmoil and chaos were relentlessly creeping closer to home, becoming an imminent threat to national, as well as personal, security.

Headlines in both small and large newspapers across America in the first decade of the twentieth century reflected the upheaval: "Radicals Want to Control All American Labor: Leaders Seeking Industrial, Economic and Political Revolution in America,"[59] "Police in Danger: Every Anarchist Who Comes to the United States Has His Stack of Bombs,"[60] "Terrorizing Bomb Throwers of

Europe Now Threaten America,"[61] and "Anarchists Head Mob in Paterson Mill Riot."[62]

Even more alarming were reports that American leaders were now the targets of revolutionary assassins. Despite the open threats of Socialists, Americans were still shocked when President William McKinley was assassinated by a self-avowed anarchist in 1901. Leon Czolgosz, the son of immigrants, shot the President during a reception at the Pan-American Exposition in Buffalo, New York. For the first time, Americans began to realize that the revolution was no longer half a world away. It was right here in our own backyard.

If McKinley's assassination had been an isolated incident, it would have been bad enough. But it was followed in subsequent years by a series of bombings, setting Americans even further on edge. In 1905, the former governor of Idaho, who, years earlier had publicly clashed with labor unions over wage increases, was killed by suspected militant unionists in a bomb blast. Between 1906 and 1911, one-hundred-ten bombs were exploded nationwide.[63] Each perpetrator had suspected or confirmed ties to radical unions. Among the deadliest was the 1910 bombing of the *Los Angeles Times*, in which twenty innocent people were killed.[64]

The year 1919 was a particularly busy one for Socialists and anarchists. A total of thirty-eight bombs were detonated that year alone. One group of bombs was dispersed in April and another in June. The first group consisted of thirty mail bombs that were sent to prominent politicians, newspaper editors, and businessmen who had opposed anarchism. Then on June 2, eight bombs were detonated almost simultaneously in eight different cities.[65] Among the targets were the homes of John D. Rockefeller and Woodrow Wilson's newly appointed attorney general, A. Mitchell Palmer. Each of the thirty-eight bombs was accompanied by anarchist flyers.[66]

These incidents came on the heels of the Seattle General Strike of 1919, one of the most dramatic showdowns between Capitalism and Socialism in American history. A brief overview of this strike, utilizing original newspaper articles and headlines from February 1 through February 13, 1919, shows the tension that existed in America at that time. Furthermore, it explains the continuing development of the Pledge of Allegiance and the role it played helping America get through this troubled time in her history.[67]

Like most strikes, the Seattle General Strike started with a call for a wage increase—this time, for shipyard workers. Seattle was the nation's leading supplier of ships for the war effort. The unions had a contract with the government, part of which allowed its workers to receive "higher wages than those engaged in similar work anywhere."[68] In the contract, the unions agreed not to strike, but "to adjust all differences, inclusive of wages" through the Shipping Board, the regulatory agency for the shipyards.[69]

Inflation on the West Coast was higher than in other parts of the country, argued the unions, and an increase in pay would offset the cost of living. Shipyard owners initially agreed to the increase, but only for skilled workers, not for the unskilled workers who were hardest hit by the price increases. Interpreting this as a strategic move to split the unions, the skilled shipyard workers joined their unskilled brethren and voted to strike. This action was a breach of contract, and the Shipping Board responded by threatening to withhold steel from the yard owners if *any* increase in wages was given.[70]

This incensed Seattle's labor unions, and the call went out for a general strike, a radical concept with the ultimate goal of crippling the entire nation as a means of instigating a takeover of power. Not only would all shipyard workers strike, but virtually every worker in every segment of Seattle—from barbers to garbage wagon drivers—would unite in solidarity. This would bring not only the shipping industry to its knees, but the city, as well. After that, left leaning Tacoma would follow, then the state, and ultimately, the nation.

The strike was the first step. While it was in effect, "worker committees" would take control of city services. Everything from feeding the strikers' families, to picking up the garbage, delivering milk, policing the streets, filling prescriptions, looking after the destitute, and keeping the men's beards well groomed had been organized beforehand by the union members.[71] This was a critical element to the strike's success, because it would prove that an American city could be "managed by committee," until now only a theory in the Preamble of the nation's most radical Socialist organization up to this point, the Industrial Workers of the World.[72]

"The army of production must be organized, not only for everyday struggle with capitalists, but also to carry on production when capitalism shall have been overthrown. By organizing industrially we are forming the structure of the new society . . . ." Written in 1905 at the founding of the Industrial Workers of the World Conference, this idea had never been tested. Until now. "The power of the strikers *to manage* will win this strike," declared Seattle's only union newspaper, the *Union Record*.[73]

It didn't help that *Union Record* journalist, Anna Strong, declared at the outset that the unions were ready to unleash "the most tremendous move ever made by labor in this country." Strong went on to claim this to be the strike that would bring "the closing down of the capitalistically controlled industries of Seattle, while the workers organize to . . . preserve order . . . THIS will move them, for this looks too much like the taking over of POWER by the workers."[74]

Seattle had been ripe for such a showdown for

more than a year at this point. Since the late 1890s when a colonization plan was put into effect for the specific purpose of capturing the region politically, the entire northwestern region of the United States had become a bastion of Socialism and radicalized unions.[75] But there was also a vibrant free-enterprise business community that very boldly voiced its distrust of Socialism. When the Bolsheviks won Russia, the radical element in Seattle's labor movement had been visibly energized. Fifteen months later, the business community wondered aloud if the impending strike was a ruse to start the much ballyhooed Revolution. As one businessman wrote in a full page paid advertisement intended to expose the strike leaders' motives, the union's actions had nothing to do with higher wages and everything to do with a "furtherance of the Bolshevik conspiracy."[76]

As negotiations over the wage increase broke down and a strike seemed inevitable, tension grew. "The eyes of the nation are fixed on Seattle,"[77] declared a Rotary Club member in one of many articles in the city's three privately owned newspapers that vehemently opposed the strike and attributed its origins to revolutionary Socialists.[78]

Throughout the country, entire front pages of newspapers headlined nothing but stories of revolution—either the strike in Seattle, the turmoil in Germany, the revolution in Russia, the chaos in Romania, or unrest in Britain.

On February 5, the *Seattle Star* drew a line in the sand. Underneath a banner headline that ran edge to edge, Seattle citizens were warned, "This is no time to mince words. A part of our community is, in fact, defying our government and is, in fact, contemplating changing that government, and not by *American methods*. This small part of our city talks plainly about 'taking over things,' of 'resuming under *our* management.' We call this thing that is upon us a general strike, but it is more than that. It is to be an acid test of American citizenship—an acid test of all those principles for which our soldiers have fought and died. The challenge is right up to you, men and women of Seattle . . . Under which flag do you stand?"[79]

Adding fuel to the fire, Bolshevik-themed flyers confettied Seattle streets. "There is only one way out: a nation-wide general strike with its object the overthrow of the present rotten system . . . The Russians have shown you the way out . . . the employing class must be overthrown." In the minds of local business owners, this further confirmed their suspicions that the strike was nothing less than a setup for revolution.[80]

Despite pleas from all corners of Seattle, nothing could be done to thwart the radicals' strike plans. On Thursday, February 6, at precisely 10:00 a.m., thirty thousand workers walked off their jobs, and Seattle turned into a ghost town. But by Saturday, it was crystal clear that there was no support from the general public for the strike. Quite the opposite, Seattle citizens stood their ground when a small committee of more moderate union members asked for an audience with the city's mayor. The citizens, along with the mayor, answered that they would have nothing to do with the strikers. *This community refuses to recognize or deal with revolutionists* was the message sent via the newspapers to the strikers, the nation, and the world. Just three days into it, the strike began to unravel.

It suffered through a few more days of fits and starts until it was finally relegated to the history books. For all the drama it produced, the strike fizzled an inglorious death and evaporated into oblivion. The repercussions for America's future, however, were monumental.

In the eyes of the public, the combined actions of organized labor, the relentless agitation of revolutionaries, and the endless reports of worldwide revolution were not disparate events. Rather, the sequence of revolutionary incidents over the past forty years had converged to such a point that Americans realized they were now battling Socialism in their own backyard. The Seattle Strike only confirmed that belief, especially when, after the strike, Anna Louise Strong wrote the following: "If by revolution is meant violence, forcible taking of property, the killing or maiming of men, surely no group of workers dreamed of such action. But if by revolution is meant that a Great Change is coming over the face of the world, which will transform the method of carrying on industry . . . then . . . our General Strike was one very definite step toward it . . . In place of two classes competing for the fruits of industry, there must be, eventually, ONLY ONE CLASS."[81]

Americans were left feeling vulnerable against a dangerous and persistent enemy. The Sedition Act of 1918 was supposed to have prevented the proliferation of anarchy in America. But the Seattle General Strike happened anyway. As a result, an unsatisfied citizenry either took measures into their own hands or demanded more vigilance on the part of their elected officials. The actions that followed comprise the First Red Scare, an era marked with violations of civil liberties and vigilante justice. Citizens were imprisoned for nothing more than criticizing the government, particularly America's involvement in the First World War. Laws were written that required Americans to take loyalty oaths. Some anarchists were terrorized, and the crimes were never investigated. Of the many stories from this era, one is particularly disturbing, as it represents the extent government goes to when it ignores civil rights.

A Montana farmer, Earnest Starr, refused to kiss the American flag when brought before a local committee of his fellow citizens curious about why he had not made Liberty Bond contributions. Calling the flag "nothing but a piece of cotton," he refused to kiss it. For this, he was convicted of sedition and served nearly three years of a ten-year prison sentence. (He and seventy-eight other

Montanans who were wrongly imprisoned for speech critical of the war effort or President Woodrow Wilson during this era were pardoned on May 3, 2006, by Governor Brian Schweitzer.[82])

The volumes are legion that document the inappropriate response Americans had to the very real and legitimate threat of revolution. However, what is needed now is for the balance of the story to be told. For far too long, Americans have been led to believe that the *only* legacy that came out of the Seattle General Strike was the nightmare of the First Red Scare. Such analysis is both historically inaccurate and incomplete.

In fact, there was a second line of defense that Americans implemented as a means to thwart the steady progression of Socialism. It was called Americanism, a term defined as the active promotion of America as a noble and exceptional nation. Not a perfect nation. But a nation unique in its virtue. Some left-leaning historians portray Americanism as if it was somehow an illegitimate response to the threats felt by Americans during this era. Some even go so far as to categorize it as part of the same hysterical responses that characterized the Red Scare. This is an unfair assessment. Socialism was—and still is—a threat to freedom that deserves an honest and direct response. Americanism was—and is—such a response.

The Seattle General Strike had helped Americans clarify what they were fighting against and what they were fighting for. This development is evident in the terminology used to describe the Strike. When it began, it was described as a fight between Socialism and Capitalism. However, toward the end of the Strike, it was described as a fight between Bolshevism and Americanism, two distinctly different ideas.

The general strike had also taught liberty-loving Americans that vigilance was a necessary ingredient to maintain freedom. If American values were to be passed on from generation to generation, it would have to be done purposefully. Our ancestors seemed to instinctively know that freedom was not guaranteed for the future.

Both lessons were applied when, in 1923, the newly formed American Legion invited dozens of patriotic groups to participate in the first National Flag Conference, convened to standardize and disseminate a flag code. The list of conference invitees represented a combined membership of millions throughout the nation. Many of the organizations are still actively promoting patriotism today: the Sons of the American Revolution, the Daughters of the American Revolution, and the Boy Scouts, to name a few.

The need for a uniform flag code had become a necessity by this time. James Upham had succeeded in popularizing the American flag to such a point that nearly every state and patriotic organization had its own way of saluting, displaying, and handling the flag. The First National Flag Conference would end the confusion by creating "a few simple rules and regulations to govern the use of the flag."[83]

None other than President Warren Harding opened the conference, commending the attendees for their patriotism and encouraging them to add another item to their list—promoting "The Star-Spangled Banner" as the national anthem. A mere two percent of the population knew the words to this most patriotic of songs, President Harding pointed out. It was time for America to finally adopt a national anthem.

As the conference proceeded, a woman whose name is simply recorded as Mrs. Weyman, rose to her feet and said, "Mr. Chairman, at present we pledge allegiance to 'my flag.' I would suggest that we change that and say, 'I pledge allegiance to the United States Flag.' Anyone can pledge allegiance to 'my flag' . . . What we want to do is to salute the flag of the United States."[84] This simple suggestion struck a chord among the attendees, for it demonstrated a practical way to capture the Pledge of Allegiance for America and America only. Essentially, this was a way for America to take ownership of the Pledge, thereby preventing it from being co-opted by other nations.

The motion was adopted and in 1923, the Pledge of Allegiance was recited as follows:

I pledge allegiance to the flag of the United States and to the Republic for which it stands, one nation indivisible, with liberty and justice for all.

It was recited that way for only one year.

In 1924, the same year that Adolph Hitler sat in a jail cell writing *Mein Kampf*, Americans gathered for a second time at the National Flag Conference to further clarify the flag code and the Pledge of Allegiance. This time, "of America" would be added, as well.

I pledge allegiance to the flag of the United States of America and to the Republic for which it stands, one nation indivisible, with liberty and justice for all.

Mrs. Weyman had had the right idea. Anyone *can* pledge allegiance to "my flag" or even to "the flag of the United States." After all, Soviet Russia claimed to be a nation made up of "united states." But with the persistence of global threats to freedom, the American people began to realize that the American flag was symbolic of ideals that set America apart from every other nation. Taking the stance that the Pledge of Allegiance was specifically American ensured that future generations would grow up knowing that American ideals make America exceptional, not Russian ideals or Swedish ideals or any other nation's ideals. No matter how complex the world became or how besieged by alien philosophies, the simply worded Pledge of Allegiance would bring into focus the fact that America stands for noble ideals that no other nation stands for. From this time forward, the Pledge of Allegiance was considered a vital part of a growing movement to promote Americanism to upcoming generations of Americans.

The generation of children who had been the first to recite the Pledge of Allegiance in 1892 grew up to become the generation of leaders who fought America's greatest threat in the first decades of the twentieth century. Clarifying the Pledge of Allegiance at this particular moment in American history represents our foremothers' and forefathers' best efforts to face the challenge of radical Socialism, a challenge that was proving to be harder as time passed.

But one more step is left to complete the history of the Pledge of Allegiance, and it would take another generation of Americans—the Greatest Generation—to accomplish that.

*Americans combine the notion of religion and liberty so
intimately in their minds, that it is impossible to make
them conceive of one without the other.*
—Alexis de Tocqueville

"Infiltrate the churches ... discredit the Bible..."
— Communist goal #27

ONE NATION UNDER GOD

Three decades passed after the National Flag Conferences of 1923 and 1924 before the Pledge of Allegiance underwent a third, and final, change. During this thirty-year span, America fought and won the Second World War, defeating Nazi Germany and Imperialist Japan. It seemed, at least on the surface, as if America's homegrown Socialist movement had died out as well. Juxtaposed against Communism and Nazism, Socialists had a hard time convincing the world that Capitalism was evil. And besides, the grandchildren of yesteryear's radicals were now Capitalists themselves, earning tidy profits in their retirement portfolios. You had to look deeper to see that the attempt to revolutionize America was still very much alive.

During and after World War II, Soviet Russia made tremendous headway imposing Communism onto small, weak European nations. While Socialism in America seemed to have disappeared, Communism was clearly on the move around the globe.

Something else was on the move, as well. This was no longer simply about the industrial class versus the working class. The Communist/Socialist movement began to reveal a much more insidious goal. Karl Marx first wrote about it in *Das Kapital*—that is, the need to eradicate religion, which he called the opiate of the people. Almost sixty years earlier, in a speech before a mass audience of Socialists gathered in Chicago on November 18, 1900, a well-respected Socialist named George Herron proposed the same idea when he said, "Socialism has power to become its own religion. Essentially, Socialism is a religion—the religion of life and brotherhood for which the world has long waited . . . Let Socialists be true to the deeper meanings of the class struggle, and they may gather into the service of Socialism the great fund of religious purpose and passion which is now heartsick, unattached and wasted."[85] Fortunately, Herron's assertion was so absurd and radical, even his own comrades distanced themselves from it. The common sense of everyday Americans led them to simply ignore it, thinking so foreign a concept would die on its own.

But it did not die, and in 1954, it reared its ugly head with a vengeance. Socialism and Communism were out to destroy Christianity and with it, all of western civilization.

In 1946, Winston Churchill alerted Americans to this coming threat, warning us not to underestimate it. Churchill, the man who recognized tyranny better than any other leader in his day, traveled to Westminster College in Missouri to deliver what is now his famous "Iron Curtain" speech. He stated that "in a great number of countries, far from the Russian frontiers and throughout the world, Communist fifth columns are established and work in complete unity and absolute obedience to the directions they receive from the Communist center." (A fifth column is a group of people working clandestinely to invade or undermine a nation from within.) Churchill continued: "Except in the British Commonwealth and in the United States where Communism is in its infancy, the Communist parties or fifth columns constitute a growing challenge and peril to *Christian civilization* [emphasis mine] . . . we should be most unwise not to face them squarely while time remains."

Not many years later, Americans awakened to the urgency of Churchill's warning when the book *Witness* was published, exposing subversive Communist activity in the American government during the 1930s and 40s. Shortly afterward, Senator Joseph McCarthy reported that Communists had infiltrated Voice of America, the State Department, and the US Army. (McCarthy certainly over-reached in his abusive attempts to discredit many loyal Americans who simply disagreed with his politics, but his claim that Communists had infiltrated many American institutions was ultimately vindicated when the Venona papers were released in 1995.) Nevertheless, his assertions matched what the Socialists had been saying since the turn of the century—that they would bring America down by working from within its institutional and governmental structures. Despite McCarthy's eventual fall from grace and attempts to minimize Communist threats, Americans instinctively remained guarded.

It was against this backdrop that the Second Session of the 83rd Congress convened on February 8, 1954.

Following longstanding tradition, Congress opened with a prayer. There was nothing unusual about that. It was unusual, however, that Congress officially marked the date in history by recognizing the fifth anniversary of the arrest of a Hungarian Catholic priest, Cardinal Joseph Mindszenty. In 1954, Cardinal Mindszenty was known worldwide for his courageous defiance of Communism. Today, if you were to ask Americans who Cardinal Mindszenty was, you would draw blank stares. But during this era, he drew huge crowds whenever he held a Mass—so huge the streets overflowed for blocks outside the church doors. In 1949, he was on the cover of Time magazine.

This Cardinal was no stranger to persecution. During World War II, he had been imprisoned by the Nazis for resisting their takeover of Hungary's Catholic schools and for exposing Hitler's goal to obliterate the

Christian Church.

Following is a portion of Congress' opening prayer that day.

O Lord Almighty Father . . . In our prayer we join the imploring millions whose silent invocations rise to Thee from the dark dungeons of the Iron Curtain, from the most obscure corners of the slave camps, and from the horror chambers of the secret police . . . give us strength as Thou hast given strength to Thy servant, Cardinal Mindszenty. He defied the tyrant's wrath until condemned to prison five years ago today. On this anniversary . . . Bestow upon us the endowments of Thy divine benevolence that this Chamber . . . remain the fortress of man's God-given right to life, liberty and the pursuit of happiness, a beacon to dispel the dark forces of death, tyranny and the very denial of Thy Holy Name."[86]

Over the course of the next several days, the

United States Congress observed the anniversary of Cardinal Mindszenty's arrest and imprisonment with speeches about his heroism and reminders that his persecution was symbolic of the Communists' quest to eradicate Christianity from the globe. United States Congressmen from both sides of the aisle stood one after another to mark the moment in history.

Representative John McCormack, a Democrat from Massachusetts, was the first to speak: "On September 26, 1949, the newly established Ministry of People's Enlightenment announced that 'an organized struggle will begin on the ideological plane for the eradication of Capitalism.' This meant open warfare against the church and the clergy. In that struggle, the Communists were prepared to use police, prisons, guns and gallows." He went on to detail Cardinal Mindszenty's record of protesting the Communist practices of seizing church schools, teaching Marxism in government controlled schools, suppressing free speech and the "elimination of the Christian spirit from Hungarian culture."[87]

Next in line was Representative Alvin Bentley,

Republican from Michigan, who was actually in Budapest as an American diplomat when Cardinal Mindszenty was arrested, tried, and sentenced. Representative Bentley said, "the millions of people who live . . . behind the Iron Curtain can call neither their bodies nor their minds their own—the only freedom left them is that of spirit . . . and so, I ask you today, my friends, to unite with those people back there in spirit, whether they be Poles or Czechs or Slovaks or Hungarians or any other of the oppressed . . . The martyrs behind the Iron Curtain today are also giving of their blood to ensure that the Christian religion will never die . . . And while we cannot relieve their physical and their mental sufferings, we can be with them in our hearts."[88]

Representative Charles J. Kersten, Republican from Wisconsin and Chairman of the Select Committee on Communist Aggression, stood to say the following: "We in the free world can hardly believe some of the things that happen in Communist courts . . . we in the United States do not fully realize that the Soviets have instituted a systematic plan for the destruction of religion."[89]

The Republican Representative from New York,

Kenneth Keating, followed. "The most recent case that ranks with that of Cardinal Mindszenty is that of Cardinal Wyszysnki of Poland. In many respects the two cardinals have parallel positions . . . Both were courageously outspoken in their devotion to the principles of their faith, and both were looked upon as sources of inspiration to their people in resisting the atheistic doctrines of Communism."[90]

The congressional speeches spilled over to the next day. Representative Melvin Price, Democrat from Illinois said, "The entire free world paid tribute yesterday to the great religious leader, Cardinal Mindszenty . . . Recognizing the strength of religion in combating the godless ideology of Communism, the evil leaders in Hungary attempted to subdue resistance to their Red regime by persecution . . . the arrest of Cardinal Mindszenty did more than any one single thing to awaken the world to the true menace of Communism . . . The world quickly realized that the persecution of Cardinal Mindszenty was not merely the concern of the Roman Catholic Church and the Hungarian nation, but that it was the concern of freemen everywhere."[91]

Representative Barratt O'Hara, Democrat from Illinois said, "I join in this message to the silenced and oppressed people of Hungary: We will not rest in our prayers and in our efforts until Cardinal Mindszenty is free and to all the people of Hungary have been restored the blessings of liberty, the dignity of man and the right to worship God. Cardinal Mindszenty we hold to be one of the great Christian martyrs of our times. The story of his heroism under the torture of martyrdom will never die."[92]

The US Congress did more than make speeches supporting Cardinal Mindszenty. They used the occasion of the anniversary to introduce legislation to add the phrase "under God" to the Pledge of Allegiance. A joint resolution was introduced by two Michigan Congressmen, Republican Senator Homer Ferguson and Democratic Representative Louis Rabaut. Addressing the House of Representatives, Representative Rabaut stated, "The fundamental issue which is the unbridgeable gap between America and Communist Russia is a belief in Almighty God."[93]

But there's more to the story. Remarkably, the idea to add "under God" to the Pledge was the subject of a sermon given by Reverend George McPherson Docherty at the New York Avenue Presbyterian Church in Washington, D.C., just the day before. Abraham Lincoln had attended this church during his presidency. It was traditional for presidents to sit in Lincoln's pew on the Sunday closest to Lincoln's birthday. On this particular Sunday, it was President Dwight Eisenhower's turn to occupy Lincoln's seat. Reverend Docherty knew that the President would be in his congregation, and he decided to preach a sermon he had preached two years earlier. That sermon's theme was the meaning of freedom, and in it, Reverend Docherty proposed the idea that "under God" should be added to the Pledge of Allegiance.

"Freedom is a subject everyone seems to be talking about," Reverend Docherty said. "What do we mean by freedom?" He pointed out that Abraham Lincoln, in his Gettysburg Address, saw America as a nation "conceived in liberty and dedicated to the proposition that all men are created equal." The question Lincoln asks is the timeless and timely one: "whether this nation, or any nation, so conceived and so dedicated shall long endure." Reverend Docherty's next statement was almost as if he spoke for every generation of Americans. "This is the issue we face today."[94]

To Docherty, as well as to Lincoln and to millions of other Americans, both then and now, God is the defining factor that enables our nation to "long endure." Docherty reminded his congregants that Lincoln understood that "under God—this nation shall know a new birth of freedom" and that by implication, it would only be under God that "government of the people, by the people and for the people shall not perish from the earth."

As Docherty pondered for himself the same question he asked his audience that day—*What is the meaning of freedom?*—he concluded that something was missing from the Pledge of Allegiance. That something was an acknowledgment of God. "It is the one fundamental concept that completely and ultimately separates Communist Russia from the democratic institutions of this country. This was clearly seen by Lincoln. 'One nation under God—this nation shall know a new birth of freedom.'"

"Under God are the definitive words," Docherty

continued. "A freedom . . . defined by a fundamental belief in God. A way of life that sees man . . . a sentient being created by God and seeking to know His will. In this land there is neither Jew nor Greek, bond nor free, male nor female, for we are one nation indivisible under God and humbly as God has given us to see the light we seek liberty and justice for all."[95]

"The only point I make in raising the issue of the Pledge of Allegiance is that it seems to me to omit this theological implication that is inherent in the 'American Way of Life.' It should be 'one nation, indivisible, under God.' Once 'Under [sic] God' then we can define what we mean by 'liberty and justice for all.' To omit the words 'Under God' in the Pledge of Allegiance is to omit the definitive character of the American Way of Life."[96]

Reverend Docherty's sentiments mirrored what was already happening on a grassroots level around the nation. In 1948, Louis P. Bowman, Chaplain of the Sons of the American Revolution, had been assigned to lead the Pledge for his chapter at the meeting that traditionally recognized Lincoln's birthday. Preparing his remarks, he noticed Lincoln's wording in the Gettysburg Address—

"this nation under God shall have a new birth of freedom"—and decided the phrasing was a precedent worth continuing. Over the years, he encouraged other chapters to do the same. At one meeting held in 1952, a member was so inspired, he wrote to his former employer, William J. Hearst, Jr., owner of the Hearst newspaper chain, and told him about the addition.[97] The Hearst newspapers quickly became strong supporters and encouraged the grassroots campaign through editorials in its many newspapers.[98]

Meanwhile, the Knights of Columbus, a Catholic fraternal organization, had also begun reciting the Pledge with "under God" in 1951.[99] They, too, began a letter-writing campaign to make its addition official. By 1954, nearly every patriotic and veterans organization, as well as businesses and civic organizations, actively supported the idea.

Reverend Docherty's sermon was just what President Eisenhower needed to make a final decision on a bill he knew would soon come his way. The very next day, a Joint Resolution was introduced in the House by Representative Louis Rabaut and two days later by

Senator Homer Ferguson. In June, the bill was passed unanimously and soon afterward, signed into law.

Since June 14, 1954, Flag Day, Americans have recited the Pledge of Allegiance as follows:

I pledge allegiance

to the flag of the United States of America

and to the republic for which it stands,

one nation under God,

indivisible,

with liberty and justice for all.

The legacy of the Pledge of Allegiance—not just its inspiring words, but the rich history that crafted those words—has finally been told. Now, it is our responsibility to ensure that it is passed along to future generations.

Even more importantly, it falls on our shoulders to continue the fight to protect our God-given freedom. The struggle to protect the Pledge is essentially the struggle to protect freedom: freedom of expression, freedom of thought, freedom of religion.

It is that concept—the concept of freedom—that lifts America above every other nation that has ever existed since civilization began.

However, the concept of freedom is constantly threatened. Before the Civil War, slavery threatened to remake freedom into something unrecognizable, a mockery of what it was meant to be. In 1888 and throughout the first decades of the twentieth century, Socialism threatened to infect freedom by replacing the promise of equal opportunity with the deception of equal results. In 1954, Communism threatened to deal the final blow to freedom by replacing God with government. At every turn, Americans squared off against these threats and fought them back as if their lives and their children's lives depended on it. For, indeed, what is life without freedom?

It is now this generation's turn to protect the blessings of freedom.

I pledge allegiance to the flag of the United States of America, and to the republic for which it stands, one nation, under God, with liberty and justice for all.

Do away with all loyalty oaths.

— Communist goal #13

SEVEN

THE PLEDGE AND AMERICA'S FUTURE

The Pledge of Allegiance has undergone an increasing number of attacks in recent years as various groups and individuals attempt to minimize its importance or eliminate it entirely from the fabric of American life. In 2010, an Arlington High School student, in Arlington, Massachusetts, made national news when school officials denied his petition to allow easy access for students to voluntarily recite the Pledge.[100] Months later, FoxNews reported that a political group in Brookline, Massachusetts, called Brookline Political Action for Peace (PAX), pushed for a school policy to send students home with permission slips for parents to sign before they were allowed to recite the Pledge.[101] At a 2010 debate in the 8th Congressional District in Illinois, a League of Women Voters moderator tried to ignore requests from the audience to recite the Pledge of Allegiance before starting their meeting.[102] In June, 2011, news outlets reported County Judge Sterling Lacy in Bowie County, Texas, attempted to remove from the official minutes of court business the recitation of the Pledge and the daily prayer.[103]

In each of these cases, a firestorm of controversy erupted as millions of Americans voiced their indignation and anger. Their voices were heard. The Arlington school district eventually required every public school principal to allow children the opportunity to recite the Pledge of Allegiance.[104] In the Texas case, the judge's efforts were thwarted by County Clerk Natalie Nichols and the Pledge was reinserted into the minutes. In the case of the Illinois debate, the audience spontaneously rose to their feet and recited the Pledge despite the moderator's objections.

Attempts to chip away at the heart of the Pledge by removing "under God" have also become increasingly more frequent and more brazen. Among the most serious of these attempts was a recent court case challenging its constitutionality. The case was brought in 2000 when a self-described atheist, Michael Newdow, sued the Elk Grove school district on behalf of his daughter, arguing she was being forced to acknowledge God during the school's daily recitation of the Pledge. In legal terms, Newdow argued that "under God" is an endorsement of religion and therefore, in violation of the Establishment Clause.[105] In 2002 the Ninth Circuit Court of Appeals agreed with him—"under God" in the Pledge of Allegiance was unconstitutional.

Americans were outraged. The infamous 9/11 attacks had occurred between the time that Newdow sued and the Ninth Circuit's decision, placing his challenge squarely in the spotlight of a nation whose patriotism had been re-energized. Americans considered Newdow's challenge to be not only a personal affront, but also a slap in the face of every man and woman who would risk their lives to defend freedom. In polls conducted by *Newsweek* and *The Washington Post* in June, 2002, just days after the ruling, nearly ninety percent favored keeping "under God" in the Pledge of Allegiance. ABC News also conducted a poll that showed eighty-four percent favored keeping the phrase.[106]

To some, it might seem as if those overwhelming numbers were nothing more than a reflection of pumped-up patriotism after 9/11. But such an analysis would not explain another poll asking the same question seven years later. In 2008, Rasmussen asked one thousand likely US voters if "under God" should remain in the Pledge. Again, the response was overwhelming—eighty-two percent said yes.[107]

In 2004, on Flag Day no less, the nation breathed a collective sigh of relief upon hearing that Newdow had lost his case. The Pledge was saved from a change most Americans did not want. But there was a downside to the ruling. The Supreme Court had based its decision on legal procedure rather than on the merits of the case. Newdow did not have standing to bring the case into the judicial system because he was a non-custodial parent. In essence, the Supreme Court's refusal to argue the merits of the case virtually guarantees that there will be another attempt to remove "under God" at some point in the future.

In 2011, the barrage of attacks on the Pledge of Allegiance seems unending. Besides the Texas controversy mentioned earlier, Brookline, Massachusetts, reasserted itself in the news by proposing that the Pledge be removed completely from schools. Just days before the tenth anniversary of 9/11, leader Martin Rosenthal said it made his "skin crawl" to think of the pressure put on children to recite it. He also said the Pledge had "no educational value."[108]

It was NBC, however, that caught the brunt of national ire in June, 2011, when it ran the opening segment of the U.S. Open Golf Championship with a patriotic montage that included soldiers, flags, and the much-beloved Pledge of Allegiance. The imagery was quite patriotic, until the children reciting the Pledge reached the point of the recitation that included "under God." At that exact moment, the camera cut to another image, leaving "under God" on the cutting room floor. Presto! Another instance of the Pledge minus "under God." The American public was in no mood to tolerate another such insult and began Twittering their frustration immediately. NBC defended the incident by claiming it was an oversight by the editors. But the disapproval was so swift and overwhelming, NBC execs apologized, both during the program and later in a letter to Congress.[109]

No sooner had the NBC debacle settled down that Americans learned of another Pledge controversy brewing at City Hall in Eugene, Oregon. City Councilman Mike Clark proposed a measure to recite the Pledge prior to every city council meeting, a tradition that most Americans happily participate in. Clark's motivation was to demonstrate to his more conservative constituents that their values are appreciated, too, especially in a city that so loudly touts its tolerance of diversity. Yet apparently, tolerance ends when it concerns patriotic traditions because the council voted down the measure. One councilman said the Pledge of Allegiance "had no place at City Hall." Eugene's mayor said it was "divisive." Councilman Clark said it was ironic to see "those who have championed the idea of tolerance be less tolerant on this question."

A compromise was proposed. Instead of reciting the Pledge before every meeting, it would only be recited prior to meetings with dates closest to four patriotic holidays—July Fourth, Veteran's Day, Memorial Day, and Flag Day. Unbelievably, the Fourth of July came and went, without any recitation of the Pledge. It was said that the issue was "still too hot to handle."[110]

What should Americans surmise about these cases, not only from the perspective of their increasing frequency, but also because they coincide with an unending array of attempts to purge God from our national culture, as well? Is it mere coincidence that the political conflicts dividing Americans today are accompanied by unrelenting attempts to transform America into a secularized nation? Have the two warring ideologies that began in earnest when Bellamy's novel and Upham's flag campaign walked onto the stage of American history finally reached the epicenter of the battle? Most importantly, will this generation of Americans defeat the greatest threat to freedom that exists, or at the very least stop its progress so that another generation can restore the foundations of freedom?

I believe that the fight to defend the Pledge of Allegiance <u>as it is currently written and recited</u> is a leading indicator of how these questions will be answered and thus, will play a critical role in determining our nation's future. Ronald Reagan put it succinctly when he said, "If we ever forget that we are one nation under God, then we will be a nation gone under."[111]

President Reagan's insight reflects a very basic concept—the concept that God and freedom are inseparable. There cannot be one without the other. Where there is God, there is freedom. Where there is freedom, there is God. But freedom is as fragile now as a crust of snow on a warm day. And "under God" in the Pledge of Allegiance is only one Supreme Court decision away from disappearing.

How can we, as ordinary citizens, defend this time -honored vow that is joined so intimately to our past, while at the same time is tied so steadfastly to our future?

One way is to insist that it is recited at civic meetings, political debates, athletic functions, and a host of other public events. This is a critical part of maintaining the American culture. As Professor Allen C. Guelzo stated at the dedication of a statue of Abraham Lincoln at Hillsdale College on May 8, 2009, "Political systems, whether constitutional regimes or political parties, rest on a bedrock of culture—of certain shared assumptions, rituals and unexamined attitudes … composed in equal parts of practical results and constant reminders." Winston Churchill put it this way, "A love for tradition has never weakened a nation, indeed, it has strengthened nations in their hour of peril." In other words, repeating the Pledge of Allegiance regularly will strengthen the nation because it reminds us of our common values.

Kudos for the audience members who stood up to recite the Pledge in Illinois, to the high school student who petitioned the school board to have it recited in his school, to the County Clerk who defended its inclusion in the historical record and for the City Councilman for bringing up the issue.

Another action we can take is to share the rich and unique history of the Pledge, which has been hidden far too long on dusty library shelves. This, too, is critical to our national strength because a nation that does not continually renew its values by teaching its history to each successive generation is a nation that will ultimately cease to exist. The Pledge of Allegiance—both its words *and its history*—gives us a platform to reaffirm those values and pass along America's heritage to the next generation. Whether it survives the passage of time is *our* challenge— to teach another generation of Americans the knowledge that it is God who blesses America with the gift of liberty, that our forefathers and foremothers were inspired by Christian principles to create our government, and that without God as part of our national culture, freedom will ultimately be lost.

We must create a groundswell of voices to teach our youngsters that the history of the Pledge of Allegiance is the history of America's rejection of Socialism or, for that matter, any other oppressive form of government. History shows that each time Socialism pushed forward to revolutionize America, wise and patriotic men and women made sure the cry of freedom was loud enough to push it back. Every other generation of Americans drew a line in the sand to prevent Socialism's growth in this country. This generation should do no less, beginning with the commitment that the Pledge of Allegiance will remain an important part of our children's education and will remain intact in its wording.

Finally, we can rally around the Pledge of Allegiance as the unrelenting voice of freedom in America and the world. The American flag is the visual symbol of freedom and the Pledge of Allegiance is the voice of freedom. When Americans vow their loyalty to the American idea of "liberty and justice for all," the world takes notice.

The history of Socialism in America and the history of the Pledge of Allegiance are like train tracks, both running the course of time over the landscape of multiple generations. Where will the track end? In the land of governmental control over individuals where there will be liberty and justice for no one? Or in the land of individual freedom rooted in the rule of law, where Americans will continue to strive for the promise of liberty and justice for all?

Only time will tell.

ACKNOWLEDGEMENTS

First and foremost, I thank my family, my inspiration and strength. Thank you for standing by my side and providing support. May God's richest blessings follow you all the days of your lives.

I also want to thank Kathy Rhodes for her patient editing and for challenging me to really think about choosing the words that best express my thoughts. Also, thank you, Gloria, for believing in me and for loving America. Your support means more than you know. Thanks, E.W., for urging me to follow my dream and for sharing your incredible wisdom.

APPENDIX

Prayer before the Senate

Msgr. Bela Varga, President of the

Hungarian National Council

February 8 , 1954

O Lord Almighty Father, protector of the weak and ruler of the strong, Thy humble servants lift their prayer to Thee.

In our prayer we join the imploring millions whose silent invocations rise to Thee from the dark dungeons of the Iron Curtain, from the most obscure corners of the slave camps, and from the horror chambers of the secret police. Hear these prayers, O Lord, and deliver them from evil.

O Lord give us strength as Thou hast given strength to Thy servant, Cardinal Mindszenty. He defied the tyrant's wrath until condemned to prison 5 years ago today. On this anniversary help us to dedicate ourselves with renewed firmness and a sure hope to work for Thy peace on earth and for Thy love among men.

On this anniversary, standing in this might bastion of freedom's strength, we invoke Thy providence, O Ruler of Nations, that we may justify the confidence of millions of Thy children, who are now bent but unbroken under the scourge of despotism and in the darkness of slavery. Have mercy on them and let us be led by Thy mighty hand that we may strengthen their unquenchable hope to see the end of all tyranny.

We entreat Thee, O Father in Heaven, lend Thy wisdom in all our deliberations and extend the light of Thy grace when we ponder the fate of centuries to come. Bestow upon us the endowments of Thy divine benevolence that this Chamber, that this Capitol remain the fortress of man's God-given right to life, liberty, and the pursuit of happiness, a beacon to dispel the dark forces of death, tyranny, and the very denial of Thy Holy Name.

Almighty Creator who hast made all men in Thine image and likeness free, give us strength to drive out the abominations of tyranny which defile Thy kingdom on earth.

God bless you all. Amen.

REMARKS TO CONGRESS
SENATOR HOMER FERGUSON
FEBRUARY 10, 1954

I believe this modification of the Pledge is important because it highlights one of the real fundamental differences between the free world and the Communist world, namely, belief in God.

Our Nation is founded on a fundamental belief in God, and the first and most important reason for the existence of our Government is to protect the God-given rights of our citizens.

Communism, on the contrary, rejects the very existence of God.

Spiritual values are every bit as important to the defense and safety of our Nation as are military and economic values. America must be defended by the spiritual values which exist in the hearts and souls of the American people. Our country cannot be defended by ships, planes, and guns alone.

In fact, we have an infinite lead over the communists, in terms of our spiritual and moral values because of our firm belief in God, and because of the spiritual bankruptcy of the Communists.

Indeed, Mr. President, over one of the doorways to this very Chamber inscribed in the marble are the words, "In God we trust." unless those words amount to more than a carving in stone, our country will never be able to defend itself. Those words must have a very real meaning in the heart of every American.

REMARKS TO CONGRESS
CONGRESSMAN LOUIS C. RABAUT
AUGUST 20, 1954

... one of our most devoted and articulate American patriots once said that what we obtain too cheaply we esteem to lightly. May we, as present-day Americans, never forget our sacred traditions and the incomparable and religious nature of our heritage. "Under God" in the Pledge of Allegiance to the flag expresses, aptly and forcefully, a grateful nation's attitude of dependence upon Almighty God. Certainly the spirit of the change should inspire and permeate every loyal citizen, no matter how humble or great his origin.

For under God this Nation lives.

My reason for introducing this resolution may be briefly stated. The most fundamental fact of this moment of history is that the principles of democratic government are being put to the test. The theory as to the nature of man which is the keystone in the arch of American Government is under attack by a system whose philosophy is exactly the opposite. This conflict may be waged with the material implements of war, either hot or cold, but ultimately it will be won by the system of government which is founded upon true and lasting principles, and whose people cling to those principles regardless of the sacrifices entailed. "We are a religious people," said Mr. Justice Douglas, of the United States Supreme Court, in a recent decision "whose institutions presuppose a Supreme Being." This is true in a very fundamental sense. Our political institutions reflect the traditional American conviction of the worthwhileness of the individual human being. That conviction, in turn, is based on our belief that the human person is important because he has been created in the image and likeness of God and that he has been endowed by God with certain inalienable rights which no civil authority may usurp. These principles of the worthwhileness of the individual human being are meaningless unless there exists a Supreme Being.

That is why, in four separate places in our Declaration of Independence the fathers of our Nation referred to God, justifying, by the law of nature and nature's God, the aspiration of the Thirteen Colonies to the status of an independent nation, invoking the Supreme Judge of the world to determine the rectitude of their actions, and seeking the blessings of divine providence on their undertaking. Truly, therefore, this Nation is founded under God.

… Now, in our pledge of allegiance to the flag, we salute the symbol of this Republic, and I think it most proper that this pledge express everything for which this Republic stands. The pledge is a reaffirmation of our love of country, of our devotion to an institution that finds its origin and development in the moral law and commands our respect and allegiance so long as it provides that "liberty and justice for all" in which free men can work out their own immortal destinies.

… You know and I know that the Union of Soviet Socialist Republics would not, and could not, while supporting the philosophy of communism, place in its patriotic ritual an acknowledgement that their nation existed under God. Indeed, the one fundamental issue which is the unbridgeable gap between America and Communist Russia is belief in Almighty God. By the addition of the phrase "under God" to the pledge of allegiance the consciousness of the American people will be more alerted to the true meaning of our country and its form of government. In this full awareness we will, I believe, be strengthened for the conflict now facing us and more determined to preserve our precious heritage. More importantly, the children of our land, in the regular recitation of the pledge in school, will be daily impressed with a true understanding of our way of life and its origins. As they grow and advance in this understanding, they will assume the responsibilities of self-government equipped to carry on the traditions that have been given to us. Fortify our youth in their allegiance to the flag by their dedication to one nation under God.

REMARKS TO CONGRESS

SENATOR ALEXANDER WILEY

MAY 4, 1954

... I now ask unanimous consent that the text of the Milwaukee Sentinel editorial entitled "Under God" be printed at this point in the body of the Record.

There being no objection, the editorial was ordered to be printed in the Records, as follows:

UNDER GOD

The news has been running so deep and fast lately that it took a letter from a reader published this week in the *New York Journal-American* to call attention to an idea that deserves support. In fact, the Hearst newspapers are going to make a campaign for it, and are grateful for the suggestion.

It concerns a resolution introduced by Senator Homer Ferguson, Michigan Republican, to add the words "under God" to the pledge of allegiance to the flag of the United States. As amended, the pledge would read:

"I pledge allegiance to the flag of the United States and to the Republic for which it stands, one Nation, indivisible, under God, with liberty and justice for all."

The letter to the editor, from Margaret Dunkee of New York, stated: "Here is a wonderful opportunity for all Americans to support a worthy change."

The resolution is now before the Senate Judiciary Committee. It is similar to one introduced last year by Representative Louis C. Rabaut, Democrat, of Michigan, and unless we can get some action ther Ferguson resolution, like the Rabaut one, is likely to die in committee.

It seems to us that in times like these when Godless communism is the greatest peril this Nation, faces, it becomes more necessary than ever to avow our faith in God and to affirm the recognition that the core of our strength comes from Him.

This Nation won its freedom under God. It has fought for and preserved that freedom under God. And it will continue to preserve and cherish it, with God's help.

Hence, it is fitting that those two profoundly meaningful words "under God" should be included in the pledge of allegiance so that we and our children, who recite the pledge far more often than adults, may be reminded that spiritual strength derived from God is the source of all human liberty.

Prayer Offered by Reverend Walter A. Mitchell, Pastor of Fountain Memorial Baptist Church in Washington, D. C. on June 14, 1954, the Day the Pledge of Allegiance was Recited for the First Time with the Phrase, "under God"

Our loving Heavenly Father, we praise Thee for all the wonderful memories of what this Flag Day stands for in the life of our country. May the flag of our great Nation continue to wave as an emblem of freedom, democracy and Christian principles upon which our beloved Nation has been founded.

Our gracious Father, let these days be days when all Members of this House shall personally dedicate their very best to the tremendous task to which they have been called. And let this be a time when, on the right hand and on the left, men and women shall honestly and sincerely seek to know and to do the will of God in every responsibility.

Teach us the courage of patience, the strength of endurance, and the real power of self restraint as is admonished in the Scriptures.

Let us lay aside every weight and the sin which doth so easily beset us and let us run with patience the race that is set before us, looking unto Jesus the author and finisher of our faith.

In whose name we pray. Amen.

President Eisenhower issued the following statement when he signed the bill adding "under God" to the Pledge of Allegiance

From this day forward, the millions of our school children will daily proclaim in every city and town, every village and rural school house, the dedication of our nation and our people to the Almighty.

To anyone who truly loves America, nothing could be more inspiring than to contemplate this rededication of our youth, on each school morning, to our country's true meaning.

Especially is this meaningful as we regard today's world. Over the globe, mankind has been cruelly torn by violence and brutality and, by the millions, deadened in mind and soul by a materialistic philosophy of life. Man everywhere is appalled by the prospect of atomic war.

In this somber setting, this law and its effects today have profound meaning. In this way we are reaffirming the transcendence of religious faith in America's heritage and future; in this way we shall constantly strengthen those spiritual weapons which forever will be our country's most powerful resource, in peace or in war.

ON JUNE 14, 1954 DEMOCRAT REPRESENTATIVE LESTER HOLTZMAN FROM NEW YORK INTRODUCED A RESOLUTION FOR THE HOUSE TO OPEN EACH DAY IN CONGRESS WITH THE RECITATION OF THE PLEDGE OF ALLEGIANCE

Mr. Speaker, I am today introducing in the House of Representatives a resolution which would amend the rules of the House to provide that the Pledge of Allegiance to the flag shall be made by the Members at the beginning of each day's session, immediately after the prayer by the Chaplain.

Our flag has been our inspiration since its adoption in 1777, and to us and to the peoples outside our borders it symbolizes the American way of life.

Each year on Flag Day we honor our national emblem, and once again dedicate ourselves to the ideals it represents. Our young men have fought and died on many fields to uphold the heritage of our flag, and at the moment we are engaged in a bitter fight against communism, both here and abroad. We must not, and will not, accept any foreign ideologies which would be contrary to our fundamental concepts of democracy, and which would dishonor our flag.

Many of our school children start their day with the salute to the flag, and numerous civic and patriotic organizations begin their meetings with the pledge to the flag.

We here in the House are the elected Representatives of the

people, and I believe that it would be most fitting for us to start each session with the Pledge of Allegiance, thus giving public indication of our belief in the flag, and "the Republic for which it stands." For that reason I have introduced this resolution, and I trust that it will be favorably considered by the appropriate committee.

These past few weeks it seems that we've all been hearing a lot of talk about religion and its role in politics, religion and its place in the political life of the nation. And I think it's appropriate today, at a prayer breakfast for 17,000 citizens in the State of Texas during a great political convention, that this issue be addressed.

I don't speak as a theologian or a scholar, only as one who's lived a little more than his threescore ten -- which has -- which has been a source of annoyance to some -- and as one who has been active in the political life of the nation for roughly four decades and now who's served the past three-and-a-half years in our highest office. I speak, I think I can say, as one who has seen much, who has loved his country, and who's seen it change in many ways.

I believe that faith and religion play a critical role in the political life of our nation, and always have, and that the Church -- and by that I mean all churches, all denominations -- has had a strong influence on the state, and this has worked to our benefit as a nation.

Those who created our country -- the Founding Fathers and Mothers -- understood that there is a divine order which transcends the human order. They saw the state, in fact, as a form of moral order and felt that the bedrock of moral order is religion.

The Mayflower Compact began with the words, "In the name of God,

122

Amen." The Declaration of Independence appeals to "`Nature's God'" and the "Creator'" and "the Supreme Judge of the world." Congress was given a chaplain, and the oaths of office are oaths before God.

James Madison in the Federalist Papers admitted that in the creation of our Republic he perceived the hand of the Almighty. John Jay, the first Chief Justice of the Supreme Court, warned that we must never forget the God from whom our blessings flowed. George Washington referred to religion's profound and unsurpassed place in the heart of our nation quite directly in his Farewell Address in 1796. Seven years earlier, France had erected a government that was intended to be purely secular. This new government would be grounded on reason rather than the law of God. By 1796 the French Revolution had known the Reign of Terror.

And Washington voiced reservations about the idea that there could be a wise policy without a firm moral and religious foundation. He said, "Of all the dispositions and habits which lead to political prosperity, religion and morality are indispensable supports. In vain would that man call himself a patriot who would labor to subvert these...finest props of the duties of men and citizens. The mere politician...(and) the pious man ought to respect and to cherish (religion and morality)." And he added," let us with caution indulge the supposition, that morality can be maintained without religion." I believe that George Washington knew the City of Man cannot survive without the City of God, that the -- that the Visible City will perish without the Invisible City.

Religion played not only a strong role in our national life, it played a positive role. The abolitionist movement was at heart a moral and religious movement; so was the modern civil rights struggle. And throughout this time, the state was tolerant of religious belief, expression, and practice. Society, too, was tolerant.

But in the 1960's this began to change. We began to make great steps toward secularizing our nation and removing religion from its honored place. In 1962 the Supreme Court, in the New York prayer case, banned the compulsory saying of prayers. In 1963 the Court banned the reading of the Bible in our public schools. From that point on, the courts pushed the meaning of the ruling ever outward, so that now our children are not allowed voluntary prayer. We even had to pass a law -- we passed a special law in the Congress just a few weeks ago to allow student prayer groups the same access to schoolrooms after classes that a young Marxist society, for example, would already enjoy with no opposition.

The 1962 decision opened the way to a flood of similar suits. Once religion had been made vulnerable, a series of assaults were made in one court after another, on one issue after another. Cases were started to argue against tax-exempt status for churches. Suits were brought to abolish the words "under God" from the Pledge of Allegiance and to remove "In God We Trust" from public documents and from our currency.

Today, there are those who are fighting to make sure voluntary prayer is not returned to the classrooms. And the frustrating thing for the great majority of Americans who support and understand the special importance of religion in the national life -- the frustrating thing is that those who are attacking religion claim they are doing it in the name of tolerance, freedom, and open-mindedness. Question: Isn't the real truth that they are intolerant of religion? They refuse to tolerate its importance in our lives.

If all the children of our country studied together all of the many religions in our country, wouldn't they learn greater tolerance of each other's beliefs? If children prayed together, would they not understand what they have in common? And would this not, indeed, bring them closer? And is this not to be desired? So, I submit to you that those who claim to be fighting for tolerance on this issue may not be tolerant at all.

When John Kennedy was running for President in 1960, he said that his church would not dictate his Presidency any more than he would speak for his church. Just so, and proper. But John Kennedy was speaking in an America in which the role of religion -- and by that I mean the role of all churches -- was secure. Abortion was not a political issue. Prayer was not a political issue. The right of church schools to operate was not a political issue. And it was broadly acknowledged that religious leaders had a right and a duty to speak out on the issues of the day. They held a place of respect, and a politician who spoke to or of them with a lack of respect would not long survive in the political arena. It was acknowledged then that religion held a special place, occupied a special territory in the hearts of the citizenry. The climate has changed greatly since then. And since it has, it logically follows that religion needs defenders against those who care only for the interests of the State. There are, these days, many questions on which religious leaders are obliged to offer their moral and theological guidance, and such guidance is a good and necessary thing. To know how a church and its members feel on a public issue expands the parameters of debate. It does not narrow the debate; it expands it.

The truth is, politics and morality are inseparable. And -- And as morality's foundation is religion, religion and politics are necessarily related. We need religion as a guide. We need it because we are imperfect, and our government needs the Church, because only those humble enough to admit they're sinners can bring to democracy the tolerance it requires in order to survive.

A state is nothing more than a reflection of its citizens: The more decent the citizens, the more decent the state. If you practice a religion, whether you're Catholic, Protestant, Jewish, or guided by some other faith, then your private life will be influenced by a sense of moral obligation, and so, too, will your public life. One affects the other. The churches of America do not exist by the grace of the State; the churches of America are not mere citizens of the State. The churches of America exist apart; they have their own vantage point, their own authority. Religion is its own realm; it makes its own claims.

We establish no religion in this country, nor will we ever. We command no worship. We mandate no belief. But we poison our society when we remove its theological underpinnings. We court corruption when we leave it bereft of belief. All are free to believe or not to believe; all are free to practice a faith or not. But those who believe must be free to speak of and act on their belief, to apply moral teaching to public questions.

I submit to you that the tolerant society is open to and encouraging of all religions. And this does not weaken us; it strengthens us; it makes us strong. You know, if we look back through history to all those great civilizations, those great nations that rose up to even world dominance and then deteriorated, declined, and fell, we find they all had one thing in common. One of the significant forerunners of their fall was their turning away from their God or gods. Without God, there is no virtue, because there's no prompting of the conscience. Without God, we're mired in the material, that flat world that tells us only what the senses perceive. Without God, there is a coarsening of the society. And without God, democracy will not and cannot long endure. If we ever forget that we're one nation under God, then we will be a nation gone under.

If I could just make a personal statement of my own: In these three-and-a-half years I have understood and known better than ever before the words of Lincoln, when he said that he would be the greatest fool on this footstool called Earth if he ever thought that for one moment he could perform the duties of that Office without help from One who is stronger than all.

I thank you, thank you for inviting us here today. Thank you for your kindness and your patience. May God keep you, and we -- may we, all of us, keep God.

Thank you.

MISCELLANEOUS FACTS RELATED TO
THE PLEDGE OF ALLEGIANCE

Although credit is given to Francis Bellamy as the author of the Pledge of Allegiance, we will never *really* know who created the words on the scrap of paper on page 47. Daniel Ford had a policy that no credit be given for articles in *The Youth's Companion*. Additionally, it was not expected to become what it is today—a cherished patriotic tradition.

The only possibilities are, of course, Francis Bellamy and James Upham. But because of Ford's policy, and because years went by before anyone began inquiring into its authorship, much confusion ensued. To further complicate the issue, both Upham and Ford had died before any serious investigation began.

For years, this was a major controversy, pitting the Upham family against the Bellamy family. It was Margarette Miller who first tackled the issue, writing two books on the subject that today, are considered invaluable to anyone interested in Pledge history. It wasn't until 1957 that the Library of Congress settled the issue, concluding that Bellamy was its creator.

This author has chosen to bring equal attention to both men, James Upham, for being the creator of the idea and Francis Bellamy, for giving voice to the sentiment.

The hand-over-heart salute officially replaced the raised-arm salute on June 22, 1942 when the National Flag Code became law. (Public law 77-643, Chapter 435)

The Youth's Companion was extremely popular in its day. It is mentioned by name in Laura Ingalls Wilder's book, *The Long Winter*.

The Columbian World Exposition (known today as the Chicago World's Fair) was meant to be the pre-eminent celebration for America's 400th anniversary. And it was, beyond doubt, one of the most significant events in America in the last quarter of the 1800s, if not the entire nineteenth century. The Columbian World Exposition left America a long list of first's (besides the first recitation of the Pledge of Allegiance): the first Ferris Wheel, the first Midway, and the first tastes of Cracker Jack, Juicy Fruit gum and Cream of Wheat.

The Youth's Companion was published in Boston, MA under the name of the "Perry Mason Company". Earl Stanley Gardner, author of the Perry Mason detective stories, is said to have chosen the name "Mason" because he wanted to imply a "rock-hard character". Gardner grew up in nearby Malden, MA and admits he may have subconsciously added the name, "Perry", having grown up "an enthusiastic reader of *The Youth's Companion*."

How many ways can you say Columbus Day? Apparently, the list can be never ending. Here are the many different renditions.

December, 1890	Four Hundredth Anniversary of the Discovery of America by Columbus
February, 1892	Grand National Public School Celebration
March, 1892	Columbian Public School Celebration
June, 1892	Grand Columbus National Public School Celebration
June, 1892	Columbian Celebration
September, 1892	400th Anniversary of the Discovery of America
September, 1892	Columbus Day
October, 1892	National School Celebration of Columbus Day

QUOTES

"On the diffusion of education among the people, rests the preservation and perpetuation of our free institutions."

Daniel Webster

"Our Constitution was made only for a moral and religious people. It is wholly inadequate for the government of any other."

John Adams

"In any communist country the first thing you do is wipe God or religion out of everybody's mind. The STATE becomes God and whoever's running it becomes the 'messiah'. The Left in order to ultimately succeed, has to end our understanding of God's existence and purpose; and, therefore, we're not going to fix our economic mess until we fix our moral mess. Our country is in a moral shambles, and until we fix the moral destruction that has crept over our culture, we're not going to be able to really fix anything else—and when you start talking about fixing the moral mess, then you really cause the left to rise up and come after you."

Rush Limbaugh

"I sometimes tremble to think that, although we are engaged in the best cause that ever employed the human heart, yet the prospect for success is doubtful not for want of power or of wisdom, but of virtue."

John Adams

"Every state or government that is not free is threatened by freedom."

Rush Limbaugh

"When freedom takes hold, men and women turn to the peaceful pursuit of a better life. Where freedom takes hold, hatred gives way to hope."

George W. Bush

"Patriotism is supporting your country all of the time and your government when it deserves it."   Mark Twain

"History does not long entrust the care of freedom to the weak or timid."   Dwight D. Eisenhower

"There is great need of educated men in our public life, but it is the need of educated men with patriotism."   Grover Cleveland

"Without God, there is no virtue. Without God, there is a coarsening of society."   Ronald Reagan

"There is evil and sin in the world and we are enjoined by Scripture and the Lord Jesus to oppose it with all our might."
Ronald Reagan

"For those who protect it, freedom has a taste the protected will never know."   Sgt. Michael Dang

"Whatever makes men good Christians makes men good citizens."   Daniel Webster

"There is nothing wrong with America that the faith, love of freedom, intelligence and energy of her citizens cannot cure."
Dwight D. Eisenhower

NOTES

CHAPTER 1. FOR LOVE OF LIBERTY

1. Francis Bellamy, "The Tyranny of All the People," *The Arena*, July, 1891, http://www.gutenberg.org. Accessed August, 2011.
2. William J. Murray, *The Pledge: One Nation Under God* (Tennessee: Living Ink Books, 2007), 45.
3. "Issue Years and Patent Numbers," United States Patent and Trademark Office, accessed August, 2011, http://www.uspto.gov/patents/process/search/issuyear.jsp.
4. "Table 4. Population: 1790 to 1990," US Bureau of the Census, accessed August, 2011, http://www.census. gov/population/censusdata/table-4.pdf.
5. "Table 12. Population of the 100 Largest Urban Places: 1890," US Bureau of the Census, accessed August, 2011, http://www.census.gov/ population/www/documentation/twps0027/tab12.txt.
6. "Socialist Labor Party of America," accessed August, 2011, http://www.aadet.com/article/Socialist_Labor_Party_of_America.
7. "The Social Monster," Anarchy Archives, accessed September, 2011, http://dwardmac.pitzer.edu/Anarchist_ Archives/bright/most/socialmonster.html.
8. James Green, *Death in the Haymarket: A Story of Chicago, the First Labor Movement and the Bombing that Divided Gilded Age America* (New York: Anchor Books, 2007), 95.
9. "Liberty on Violence," accessed September, 2011, http://www.webcitation.org/5v8wrPAHP.
10. "Death of Johann Most," Homicide in Chicago 1870-1930, accessed August, 2011, http://homicide.northwestern.edu/docs_fk/homicide/544/anarchist2.jpg.
11. "Strikes," accessed January, 2011, http://www.history.com/topics/strikes/page2.

12. Richard Ellis, *To the Flag* (Lawrence, Kansas: University Press of Kansas, 2005), 76.
13. "The School Flag," *The Youth's Companion*, January 23, 1890.

CHAPTER 2. FLAGS UNFURLED, PATRIOTISM RENEWED

14. "The Flag and the Public Schools," *The Youth's Companion*, January 9, 1890.
15. "The School Flag," *The Youth's Companion*, January 23, 1890.
16. Ibid.
17. Wallace Foster, *A Patriotic Primer for the Little Citizen: An Auxiliary in Teaching the Youth of Our Country the True Principles of American Citizenship*, 5th Ed. (Indianapolis: W.D. Pratt, 1909), 16.
18. Foster, *Patriotic Primer*, 16.
19. Margarette S. Miller, *I Pledge Allegiance* (Boston: The Christopher Publishing House, 1946), 84.
20. Ibid., 86.
21. Ibid., 87.
22. Ibid., 33.
23. John W. Baer, *The Pledge of Allegiance, A Revised History and Analysis*, accessed August, 2011, http:/www.oldtimeislands.org/pledge/pdgech2.htm.
24. Miller, *I Pledge Allegiance*, 27.
25. "Independent Chronicle," Answers.com, accessed August, 2011, http://www.answers.com/topic/independent-chronicle.
26. Miller, *I Pledge Allegiance*, 33-34.
27. Ibid., 79.
28. Baer, http://www.oldtimeislands.org/pledge/pdgech2.htm.
29. Francis Bellamy, "The Poetry of Human Brotherhood." Commencement address, University of Rochester, 1876.
30. Bellamy, http://www.gutenberg.org.
31. "Edward Bellamy," Wikipedia, accessed August, 2011, http://en.wikipedia.org/wiki/Edward_Bellamy.
32. John Eidsmoe, *Christianity and the Constitution: The Faith of Our Founding Fathers* (Michigan: Baker Book House Company, 1987), 38.

33. John Baer, "Chapter Three: American Socialists and Reformers," *The Pledge of Allegiance: A Revised History and Analysis*, accessed August, 2011, http://www.history.vineyard.net/pdgech3.htm.

34. Bellamy, "The Tyranny of All the People," http://www.gutenberg.org.

35. Ibid.

36. Francis Bellamy, "A New Plan for Counter-Attack on the Nation's Internal Foes: How to Mobilize the Masses to Support Primary American Doctrines, May 1, 1923," Bellamy Collection, Rush Rhees Library, University of Rochester, New York.

37. Miller, *I Pledge Allegiance*, 79.

CHAPTER 3. THE PLEDGE MAKES ITS DEBUT

38. Jeffrey Owen Jones and Peter Meyer, *The Pledge: A History of the Pledge of Allegiance* (New York: St. Martin's Press, 2010), 56-57.

39. Miller, *I Pledge Allegiance*, 108-109.

40. Ibid., 130-131.

41. Ibid., 134-135.

42. Fifty-first Congress, Session 1, 1890, 1562-1563.

43. "Coal Creek War," Wikipedia, accessed August, 2011, http://en.wikipedia.org/wiki/Coal_Creek_War.

44. "Buffalo Switchmen's Strike," Wikipedia, accessed August, 2011, http://en.wikipedia.org/wiki/ Buffalo_switchmen%27s_strike.

45. "Coeur d'Alene Idaho Labor Strike of 1892," Wikipedia, accessed August, 2011, http://en.wikipedia.org/wiki/ Coeur_d%27Alene_Idaho_Labor_Strike_of_1892.

46. "1892 New-Orleans general strike," Wikipedia, accessed August, 2011, http://en.wikipedia.org/wiki/ 1892_New_Orleans_general_strike.

47. Television documentary, National Endowment of the Humanities. http://pbs.org/. (No longer available)

48. "Homestead Strike," Wikipedia, accessed August, 2011, http://en.wikipedia.org/wiki/Homestead_Strike.

CHAPTER 4. AMERICA CELEBRATES

49. Norman Bolotin and Christine Laing, *The World's Columbian Exposition: The Chicago World's Fair of 1893* (Washington, DC: The Preservation Press, 1992), 8, 25.
50. *New York Times*, October 13, 1892.
51. *New York Times*, October 12, 1892.
52. *New York Times*, October 11, 1892.
53. "In the Schools," *New York Times*, October 22, 1892.
54. Essex Institute Historical Collections, Volume XXX (Salem, MA, 1893), 8-9.
55. "Exercises at the Celebration of Columbus Day, Friday, October 21, 1892," Lehigh University "Order of Exercises" (Bethlehem, Pennsylvania: Times Publishing Co., 1892).
56. *New York Times*, October 22, 1892.
57. *New York Times*, October 10, 1892.

CHAPTER 5. SOCIALISM – IN OUR OWN BACKYARD

58. "A Brief History of Socialism in America, January 1900," *Social Democracy Red Book* (Terre Haute, IN: Debs Publishing Co., 1900), 1-75.
59. *The Seattle Daily Times*, February 5, 1919.
60. *Chicago Eagle*, June 5, 1901.
61. *Los Angeles Times*, September 3, 1906.
62. *Washington Times*, June 19, 1902.
63. Philip S. Foner, *History of the Labor Movement in the United States, Vol. 5* (New York: International Publishers, 1999).
64. "Los Angeles Times Bombing," Wikipedia, accessed August, 2011, http://en.wikipedia.org/wiki/Los_Angeles_Times_bombing.
65. "First Red Scare," Wikipedia, accessed August, 2011, http://en.wikipedia.org/wiki/First_Red_Scare#April_1919_mail_bombs.
66. "Palmer Raids," Wikipedia, accessed August, 2011, http://en.wikipedia.org/wiki/Palmer_raids#cite_note-1.

67. Pacific Northwest Labor and Civil Rights History Project directed by Professor James Gregory (University of Washington: Harry Bridges Center for Labor Studies), accessed August, 2011, http://depts.wash.edu/ labhist/strike/ index.shtml.

68. "Real Cause of the Strike," *The Post Intelligencer*, February 1, 1919.

69. "Wage Contract Broken Declares Piez," *The Post Intelligencer,* February 2, 1919.

70. "Thursday at 10:00,"*Union Record,* February 3, 1919, 1.

71."Labor to Care for Children," accessed August, 2011, http:// depts.washington.edu/labhist/strike/images/ news/ Union_Record/SUR_19190204_P1FE.jpg; "Drivers Ready to Supply All Milk Needed," accessed August, 2011, http:// depts.washington.edu/labhist/strike/images/news/ Union_Record/SUR_19190204_P1cNE.jpg; "Labor to Maintain Order in Own Ranks," accessed August, 2011, http:// depts.washington.edu/labhist/strike/images/ news/ Union_Record/SUR_19190205_P1FE.jpg.

72. Preamble to the IWW Constitution, accessed August, 2011, IWW.com.

73. "Thursday at 10:00 a.m.," *Union Record,* February 4, 1919.

74. Ibid., February 3, 1919.

75. "A Brief History of Socialism in America," Social Democracy Red Book (Terre Haute, IN: Debs Publishing Co., 1900), 11, accessed August, 2011,http://www.cddc.vt.edu/marxists/ history/usa/parties/spusa/1900/0100-sdp-briefhistorysoc.pdf.

76. "Real Cause of the Strike," *Post Intelligencer*, February 1, 1919.

77. "Rotary Against General Strike," *Post Intelligencer*, February 6, 1919.

78. "Real Cause of the Strike," Speech to Rotary by Mayor Hansen, "An Open Letter to Organized Labor."

79. *The Seattle Star*, February 5, 1919.

80. "Rogers Blames Reds for Strike," *Post Intelligencer*, February 4, 1919.

81. *The Seattle General Strike: An Account of What Happened in Seattle, and Especially in the Seattle Labor Movement During*

the General Strike, Feb 6 – 11, 1919, History Committee of the General Strike Committee (Seattle: The Seattle Union Record Publishing Co.), 7.

82. The Montana Sedition Project, a project of the University of Montana School of Journalism, accessed August, 2011, http://www.seditionproject.net/masterspreadsheet.html.

83. National Flag Conference Minutes, June 14 – 15, 1923, 8.

84. Ibid., 118.

CHAPTER 6.   ONE NATION UNDER GOD

85. George D. Herron, "A Plea for the Unity of American Socialists: Address to a Mass Meeting of Chicago Socialists," November 18, 1900, *The International Socialist Review*, Vol. 1, No. 6, December 1900 [first publishing], 321-328, accessed August, 2011, http://marxisthistory.org/history/usa/parties/spusa/1900/1118-herron-unityplea.pdf.

86. *The Congressional Record of the United States of America: Proceedings and Debates of the 83rd Congress*, February 8, 1954, Second Session, 1423.

87. Ibid., 1513.

88. Ibid., 1516.

89. Ibid.

90. Ibid., 1517.

91. Ibid., 1585.

92. Ibid., 1597.

93. Ibid., 1700.

94. Sermon preached by Dr. George M. Docherty, New York Avenue Presbyterian Church, Sunday, February 7, 1954.

95. Ibid.

96. Ibid.

97. John W. Baer, *The Pledge of Allegiance: A Revised History and Analysis* (Annapolis, MD: Free State Press, 2007).

98. "Public Recital for New Pledge," *New Jersey Journal American*, May 23, 1954.

99. "Knights of Columbus Fact Sheet," Knights of Columbus, accessed August, 2011, http://www.kofc.org/un/en/resources/communications/pledgeAllegiance.pdf.

CHAPTER 7. THE PLEDGE AND AMERICA'S FUTURE

100. "School Officials in Mass. Town Won't Let Students Recite Pledge of Allegiance," Fox News, accessed September, 2011, http://www.foxnews.com/us/2010/06/29/ma-school-officials-wont-let-students-recite-pledge-allegiance/.
101. "Massachusetts School Issues Permission Slips for Pledge of Allegiance, Fox News, accessed September, 2011, http://www.foxnews.com/us/2010/12/22/massachusetts-school-issues-permission-slips-pledge-allegiance/.
102. "The Pledge of Allegiance," You Tube, accessed August, 2011, http://www.youtube.com/watch?v=5PXYKZj7P6o.
103. "One American's Stand for Prayer and the Pledge of Allegiance," Redstate, accessed September, 2011, http://www.redstate.com/lineholder/2011/07/21/one-americans-stand-for-prayer-and-the-pledge-of-allegiance/.
104. Arlington, accessed September, 2011, http://www.boston.com/yourtown/news/arlington/2010/07/subcommittee_recommends_pledge.html.
105. "Court Dismisses Pledge Suit," Politics on MSNBC, accessed August, 2011, http://www.msnbc.msn.com/id/5208621/.
106. "Under God in the Pledge," ProCon.org, accessed August, 2011, http://undergod.procon.org/view.resource.php?resourceID=000076#F.
107. "77% Say Children Should Say Pledge At School Every Day," Rasmussen Reports, accessed August, 2011, http:/www.rasmussenreports.com/public_content/lifestyle/general_lifestyle/november_2008/77_say_children_should_say_pledge_at_school_every_day.
108. "Group Calls to Ban Pledge of Allegiance at Massachusetts Schools, Citing No Educational Value," Fox News, Accessed September, 2011, http://www.foxnews.com/us/2011/09/08/

progressive-group-in-mass-calls-for-pledge-ban-citing-no-educational-value/.

109. NBC Apologizes for Omitting 'Under God' From Pledge During U.S. Open Broadcast," You Tube, Accessed August, 2011, http://www.youtube.com/watch?NR=1&v=Cj4ddWna2AY.

110. "Compromise on Pledge of Allegiance in Oregon Town Has Some Seeing Red," Fox News, accessed August, 2011, http://www.foxnews.com/us/2011/06/28/compromise-on-pledge-allegiance-in-oregon-town-has-some-seeing-red?.

111. President Ronald Reagan, Remarks at a Dallas Ecumenical Prayer Breakfast, delivered August 23, 1984 at Reunion Arena, Dallas, Texas.

The Communist goals at the beginning of each chapter were selected from the full list that was entered into the Congressional Record, Appendix, pp A34—A35, on January 10, 1963. The complete list contains forty-five goals. To read the complete list, simply search "Communist goals".

PHOTO CREDITS

Bibliography

Books

Allen, Leslie. *Liberty: The Statue and the American Dream.* New York: Statue of Libery-Ellis Island Foundation, Inc., 1985.

Baer, John W. *The Pledge of Allegiance: A Centennial History, 1892-1992.* Annapolis, MD: John. W. Baer, 1992.

Bolotin, Norman and Laing, Christine. *The World's Columbian Exposition: The Chicago World's Fair of 1893.* Washington, D.C.: Preservation Press, 1992.

Eidsmoe, John. *Christianity and the Constitution: The Faith of Our Founding Fathers.* Grand Rapids, MI, 1987.

Ellis, Richard, *To the Flag: The Unlikely History of the Pledge of Allegiance.* Kansas: University Press of Kansas, 2005.

Foner, Philip S. *History of the Labor Movement in the United States, Vol. 5, The AFL in the Progressive Era (1910-1915).* New York: International Publishers, 1999.

Foster, Wallace. *A Patriotic Primer for the Little Citizen, An Auxiliary in Teaching the Youth of Our Country the True Principles of American Citizenship.* Indianapolis: W. D. Pratt, Printer and Binder, 1909.

Green, James. *Death in the Haymarket: A Story of Chicago, the First Labor Movement and the Bombing that Divided Gilded Age America.* New York: Anchor Books, 2006.

Guenter, Scot M. *The American Flag, 1777-1924: Cultural Shifts from Creation to Codification.* Cranbury, NJ: Associated University Presses, Inc., 1990.

Halberstam, David. *The Fifties.* New York: Villard Books, 1993.

Jones, Jeffrey Owen and Meyer, Peter. *The Pledge, A History of the Pledge of Allegiance.* New York: Thomas Dunne Books, 2010.

Bibliography

Con't.

Miller, Donald L. *City of the Century: The Epic of Chicago and the Making of America.* New York: Touchstone, 1997.

Miller, Margarette S. *I Pledge Allegiance.* Boston: The Christopher Publishing House, 1946.

Miller, Margarette S. *Twenty-Three Words.* Portsmouth, Virgina: Printcraft Press, Inc., 1976.

Murray, William J. *The Pledge: One Nation Under God.* Chattanooga, TN: Living Ink Books, 2007.

Articles

Bellamy, Francis. "A New Plan for Counter-Attack on the Nation's Internal Woes, How to Mobilize the Masses to Support Primary American Doctrines." Unpublished. May 1, 1923. Housed at Rush Rhees Library, University of Rochester.

- - - "The Tyranny of All the People." *The Arena Magazine* (1891) 181-92. http://www.gutenberg.org

- - - "The Poetry of Human Brotherhood." Commencement speech, 1876, University of Rochester, Housed at Rush Rhees Library, University of Rochester.

ABOUT THE AUTHOR

Saving One Nation Under God, The Role of the Pledge of Allegiance in America's Fight Against Socialism is Tricia Raymond's second book. Her journey to record the history of the Pledge of Allegiance began in 1993 when she was homeschooling her two older children and wanted to use the stars on the flag to create a lesson about western expansion. It was while researching the flag that she found a footnote that documented the history of the Pledge of Allegiance. Her lesson about the flag expanded to include a lesson about the Pledge of Allegiance.

For seventeen years, while raising her family, working full time and volunteering in her community, she has returned again and again to the topic of Pledge history. In 2007, she self published her first book, written for middle school students, *America's Story: A Pictorial History of the Pledge of Allegiance.*

As time passed and the Pledge took center stage in controversial court cases and news stories, Raymond decided to revisit the topic and write another book for an adult audience. *Saving One Nation Under God* is the product of her continuing quest to enlighten and educate Americans about the rich history of one of America's most cherished traditions.

Since 2007, Raymond has spoken to various groups about the history of the Pledge of Allegiance. If you would like to invite Tricia Raymond to speak to your group, you can contact her at

libertyaloud@gmail.com

If you would like to support the effort to keep the Pledge of Allegiance the way it is recited now (with "under God"), then please join her Facebook page, Saving One Nation Under God.

CPSIA information can be obtained at www.ICGtesting.com
Printed in the USA
LVOW031003031111

253323LV00003B/4/P